COLES FAMILY IN ALBEMARLE COUNTY

(B) 1776: John II, 4,750 acres.

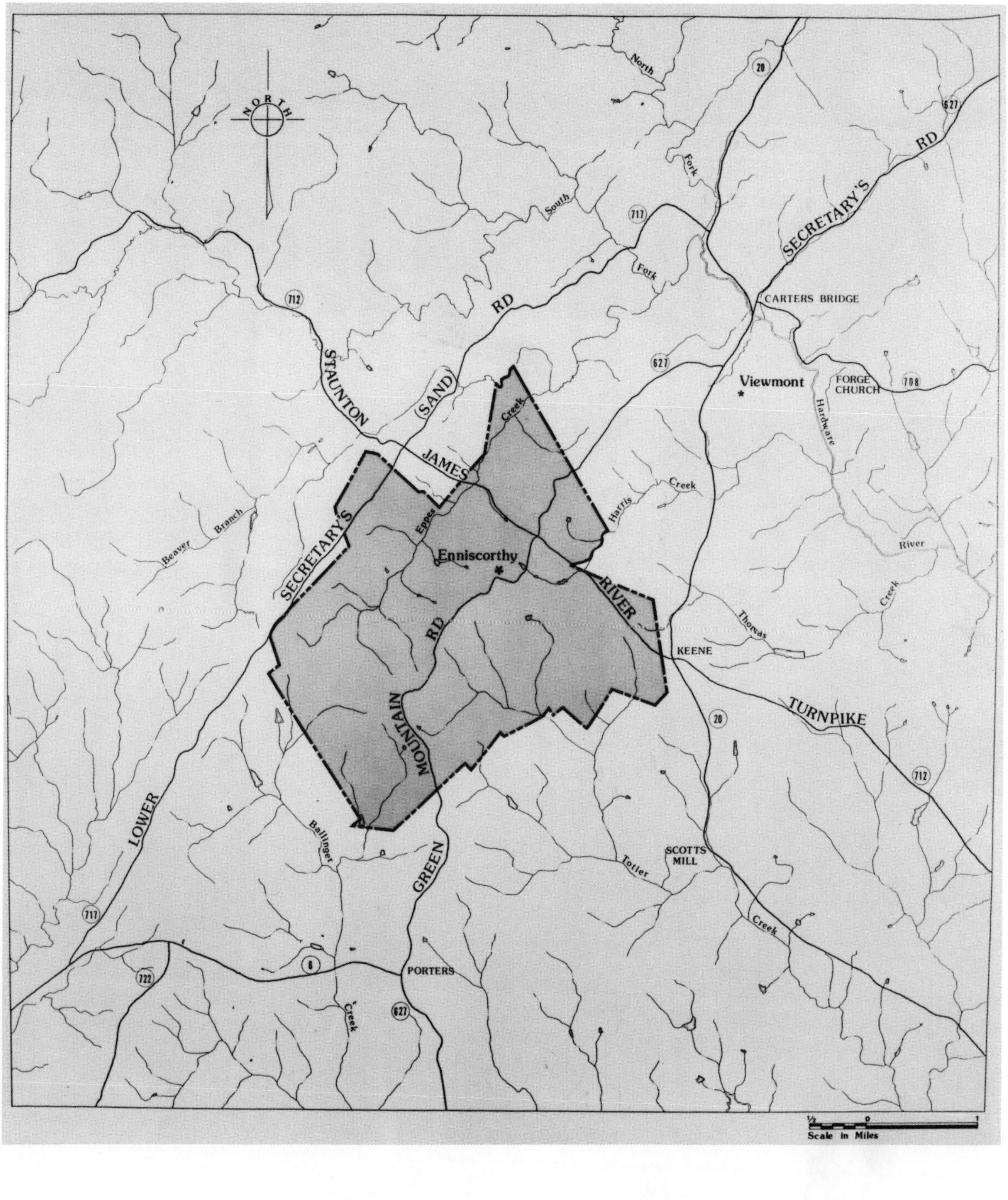

A Virginia Family and Its Plantation Houses

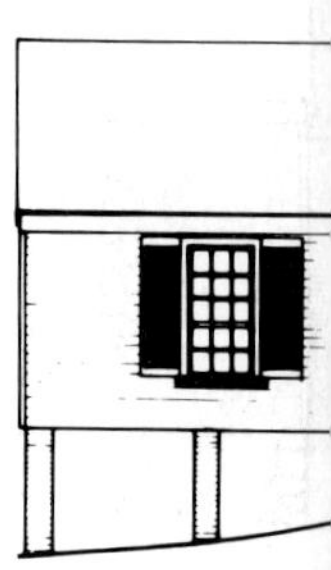

UNIVERSITY PRESS OF VIRGINIA *Charlottesville*

A VIRGINIA FAMILY
and Its
PLANTATION HOUSES

Elizabeth Langhorne
K. Edward Lay
William D. Rieley

THE UNIVERSITY PRESS OF VIRGINIA

First published 1987

Library of Congress Cataloging-in-Publication Data

Langhorne, Elizabeth Coles.
A Virginia family and its plantation houses.

Bibliography: p.
Includes index.
1. Plantations—Virginia. 2. Cole family.
3. Virginia—Biography. 4. Greek revival (Architecture)
—Virginia. 5. Neoclassicism (Architecture)—Virginia.
6. Architecture, Modern—17th–18th centuries—Virginia.
7. Architecture, Modern—19th century—Virginia.
I. Lay, K. Edward. II. Rieley, William D.
III. Title.
F227.L25 1987 975.5'03 86-28072
ISBN 0-8139-1127-3

Printed in the United States of America

To the Memory of
Bertha Lippincott Coles
and
Stricker Coles, M.D.
with love and gratitude

Contents

Foreword

Most Americans today do not realize that the interest in the history of American art and architecture is a contemporary phenomenon. Until recently, American art was regarded merely as an insignificant and derivative movement that could not be compared to the history of European and Asian culture. Given such a disparaging attitude, it is not surprising that there have been too few scholarly studies, such as this one, in the creative arts in the United States.

The Southern plantation houses considered in this book represented an economy based on land, slaves, and tobacco. Their architecture and landscapes can only be understood within the context of the enterprises and the larger economy that produced and sustained them. Present-day scholars are beginning to pay greater attention to this relation between architecture and social life, and to draw upon the full variety of records, economic and personal, private and official. This book does important, pioneering work in this approach to architectural history.

While critics often speak of Southern houses as "country houses," this is a misnomer. *Country house* refers to a very different culture. It implies that the houses were meant for weekends and summer holidays, with the principal residence in town. The truth is that the plantation house was an economic necessity. They were the brains of the plantations, and the planter's principal home. With very few exceptions, there were no town houses for the opulent. These houses were far from being elegant country houses supported by outside income.

Two of the most valuable parts of this book are the measured drawings of the houses and their gardens, many executed especially for this publication, and the account books dating from the building of the various houses that are covered here. While they conform to the general taste for the neoclassic then prevalent in the Piedmont, the Coles, in fact, added ideas of their own to make every house an individual work of art. Estouteville and Redlands also reflect the influence of their neighbor, Mr. Jefferson.

It is interesting to note that the characteristic elements of Greek architecture were originally developed in the construction of wooden temples, before construction in stone became prevalent. This meant that when Greek details were readapted to wood construction they fitted well into that material's more delicate scale. In the less sophisticated New World this was important, as the Americans did not have the stonecutters to use in any but the most important buildings.

Elements from classical architecture that were utilitarian in origin functioned as ornament when adapted to residential use in America. For example, to keep the rainwater from running down a building, a lip was provided at the end of the cornice, so the water could run down the cyma and corona, and not the face of the wall. In these plantation houses, and today in contemporary design, one sees cornices designed in this fashion, though the fireplace cornice or ceiling cornice are inside, and not related to any exterior surface.

The importance of this book lies not only in what it tells us about the houses and landscapes of one prominent Piedmont family but also in its portrayal of the life and the quality of civilization at the time. Against this rich background we can truly judge the importance of the architecture that developed in the Piedmont of Virginia.

Frederick Doveton Nichols
August 1986

Acknowledgments

Our first and most important source, and indeed the original inspiration for the present work, is *The Coles Family of Virginia*, by William B. Coles (1931). In addition we are grateful for the copies of letters made by Bertha L. Coles from a collection no longer available to the public. The splendid collections at the manuscript department of the University of Virginia's Alderman Library have always been open to us, and their staff have been more than helpful and courteous in support of our research.

We should like to thank especially the present owners of the houses treated here, for without their hospitality there could have been no book. Appropriate credit has been given elsewhere to the draftsmen and draftswomen whose drawings and site plans have added so much to its beauty and usefulness and to the owners of the many Coles portraits reproduced in these pages.

Individual thanks should go to Roberts Coles, who helped us to ascertain Coles property lines throughout the years; to Mildred Abraham of the rare books department of the Alderman Library; to Richard Collins of the Institute for Environmental Negotiations for his help in support of the early research connected with our project; to Bernard Caperton, Robert Self, and others who have contributed in more ways than it is possible to mention here. We have enjoyed the help of John Coles Langhorne, whose interests run parallel to ours, and we wish to thank our expert typist, Joan Baxter, who gave valuable time and skill to the ever-changing manuscript.

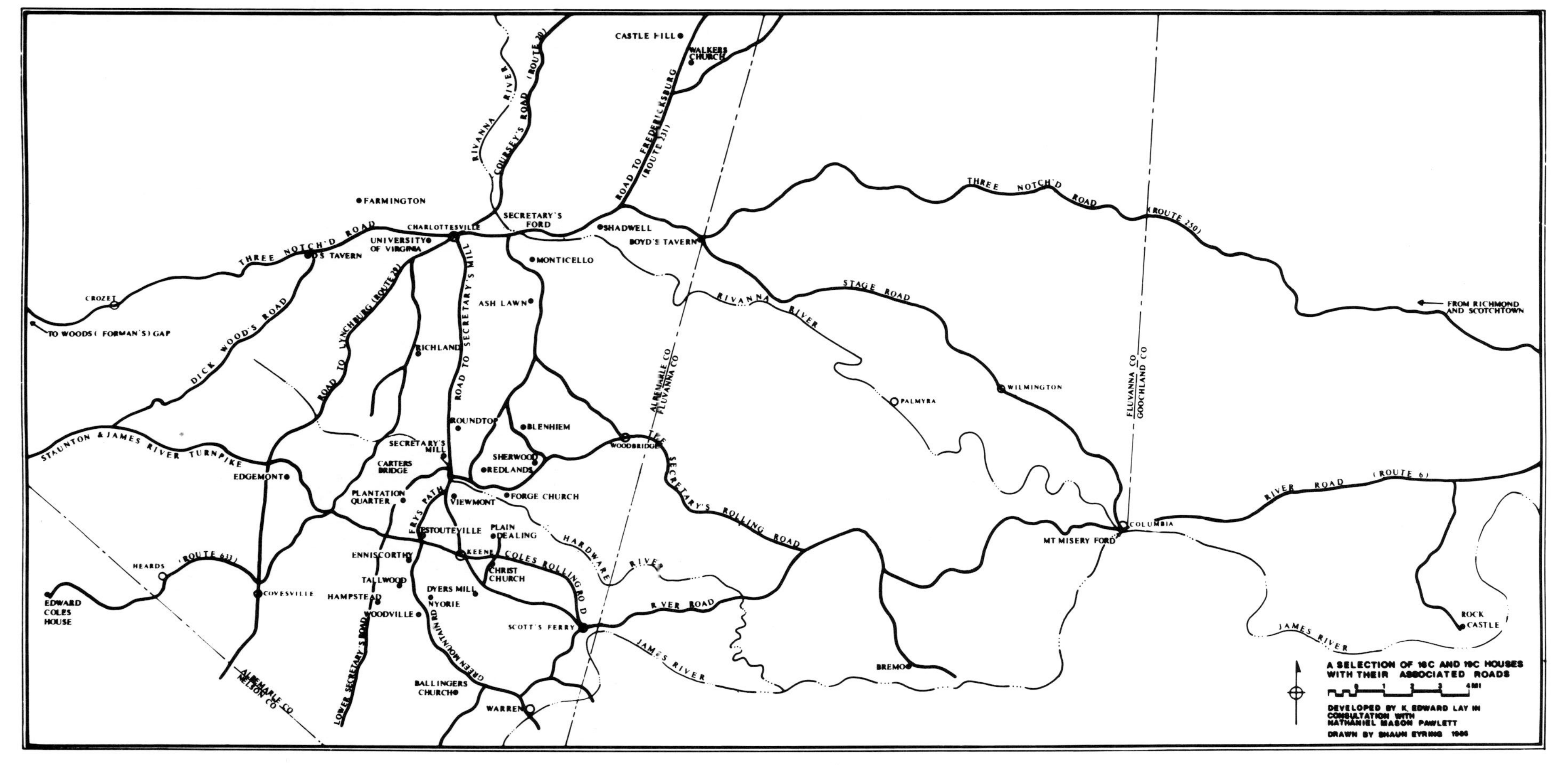
A SELECTION OF 18C AND 19C HOUSES
WITH THEIR ASSOCIATED ROADS
0 1 2 3 4MI
DEVELOPED BY K. EDWARD LAY IN
CONSULTATION WITH
NATHANIEL MASON PAWLETT
DRAWN BY SHAUN EYRING 1986
CASTLE HILL
WALKERS CHURCH
RIVANNA RIVER
COURSEY'S ROAD (ROUTE 20)
ROAD TO FREDERICKSBURG (ROUTE 231)
FARMINGTON
SECRETARY'S FORD
CHARLOTTESVILLE
SHADWELL
BOYD'S TAVERN
THREE NOTCH'D ROAD (ROUTE 250)
UNIVERSITY OF VIRGINIA
THREE NOTCH'D ROAD
MONTICELLO
CROZET
TO WOODS (FORMAN'S) GAP
ASH LAWN
STAGE ROAD
FROM RICHMOND AND SCOTCHTOWN
RIVANNA RIVER
DICK WOOD'S ROAD
ROAD TO LYNCHBURG (ROUTE 29)
RICHLAND
ROAD TO SECRETARY'S MILL
ALBEMARLE CO
FLUVANNA CO
FLUVANNA CO
GOOCHLAND CO
WILMINGTON
PALMYRA
ROUNDTOP
BLENHIEM
WOODBRIDGE
STAUNTON & JAMES RIVER TURNPIKE
SECRETARY'S MILL
CARTERS BRIDGE
SHERWOOD
REDLANDS
THE SECRETARY'S ROLLING ROAD
EDGEMONT
PLANTATION QUARTER
FRYS PATH
VIEWMONT
FORGE CHURCH
RIVER ROAD (ROUTE 6)
ESTOUTEVILLE
PLAIN DEALING
HARDWARE RIVER
COLUMBIA
MT MISERY FORD
ENNISCORTHY
KEENE
COLES ROLLING ROAD
HEARDS
(ROUTE 631)
CHRIST CHURCH
TALLWOOD
EDWARD COLES HOUSE
COVESVILLE
HAMPSTEAD
DYERS MILL
NYORIE
WOODVILLE
RIVER ROAD
SCOTT'S FERRY
GREEN MOUNTAIN RD
ROCK CASTLE
JAMES RIVER
JAMES RIVER
BREMO
ALBEMARLE CO
NELSON CO
LOWER SECRETARY'S ROAD
BALLINGERS CHURCH
WARREN

Set within the land is the dwelling—made by human hands to hold human life. . . . It fills the past, . . . it gives the present meaning; it provides for a future: the house is the physical form, the evidence *that we have lived, are alive now; it will be evidence some day that we were alive once, evidence against the arguments of time and the tricks of history.*

Eudora Welty

Introduction

As a young man in Williamsburg Thomas Jefferson took the trouble to execute measured drawings of the Governor's Palace. Fortunately this record, combined with the Bodleian prints at the Oxford University Library, has made possible the reconstruction of the Palace, so important in the history of the colonies. The importance of such preservation, of course, goes beyond the historic record. We may place an equal value on the great country houses of the plantation period in Virginia. It has been said that the country house is the greatest contribution made by England to the visual arts[1]; the same thing may be said in America of houses of the eighteenth and early nineteenth centuries. Many of these houses are works of art, and many have been recorded in appropriate detail through architectural studies, but the architectural record never really stands alone.

In this study we shall treat in detail some twelve houses, built and occupied by four generations of one Virginia family. (See fig. 1.) Starting with the Richmond house of the emigrant John Coles I, we will proceed to the houses built in Albemarle County by John Coles II and his numerous children. The first Enniscorthy, named after the town in Ireland from which the family came, has not survived, although another Enniscorthy now stands on the same site. Other houses remain, a fine legacy in this area of south Albemarle. They are survivals of a vanished culture. Today they play a necessarily limited role; they are no longer the social and economic centers dominating the close-knit neighborhoods of their own time.

It is in this original and essential role that they will appear in the following pages. We will take an extended view, looking at the complex of plantation buildings, slave quarters, and garden. All this is set in a pattern of roads, cultivated fields, barns, and streams. There, laid

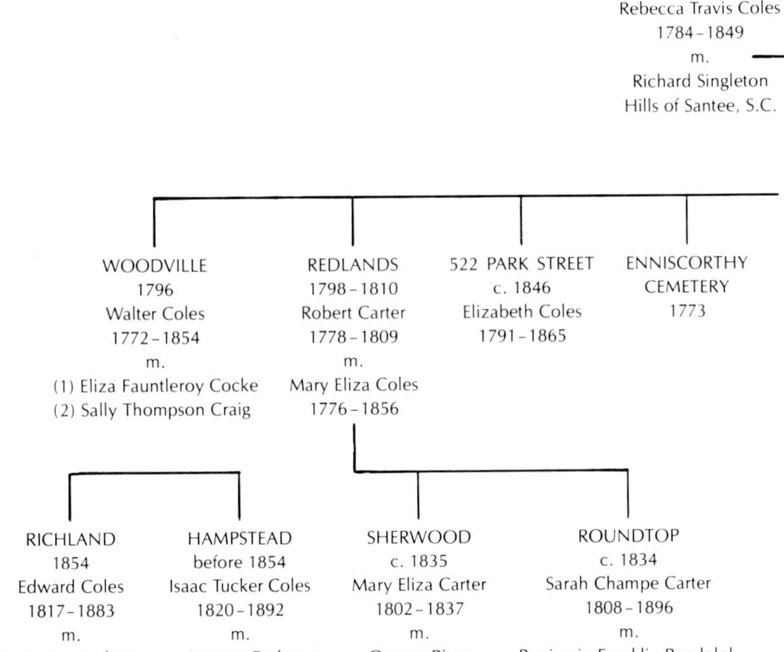

out before us, is the social and economic background of the house itself. We will indeed consider architecture, how, in successive periods, the planter raised the roof that must shelter him and his family, but the pattern we are looking at demands a wider view. Out of what social economic background did the house itself come?

We have addressed these aspects through the work of the three authors represented in our text. Professor Lay has supervised the measured drawings of the principal houses, and he has contributed the detailed analysis upon which the architectural study is based. A study of the intimate relation of each house with landscape and the various site plans has been Professor Rieley's contribution. Elizabeth Langhorne's task as writer has been to fill in the social background and to

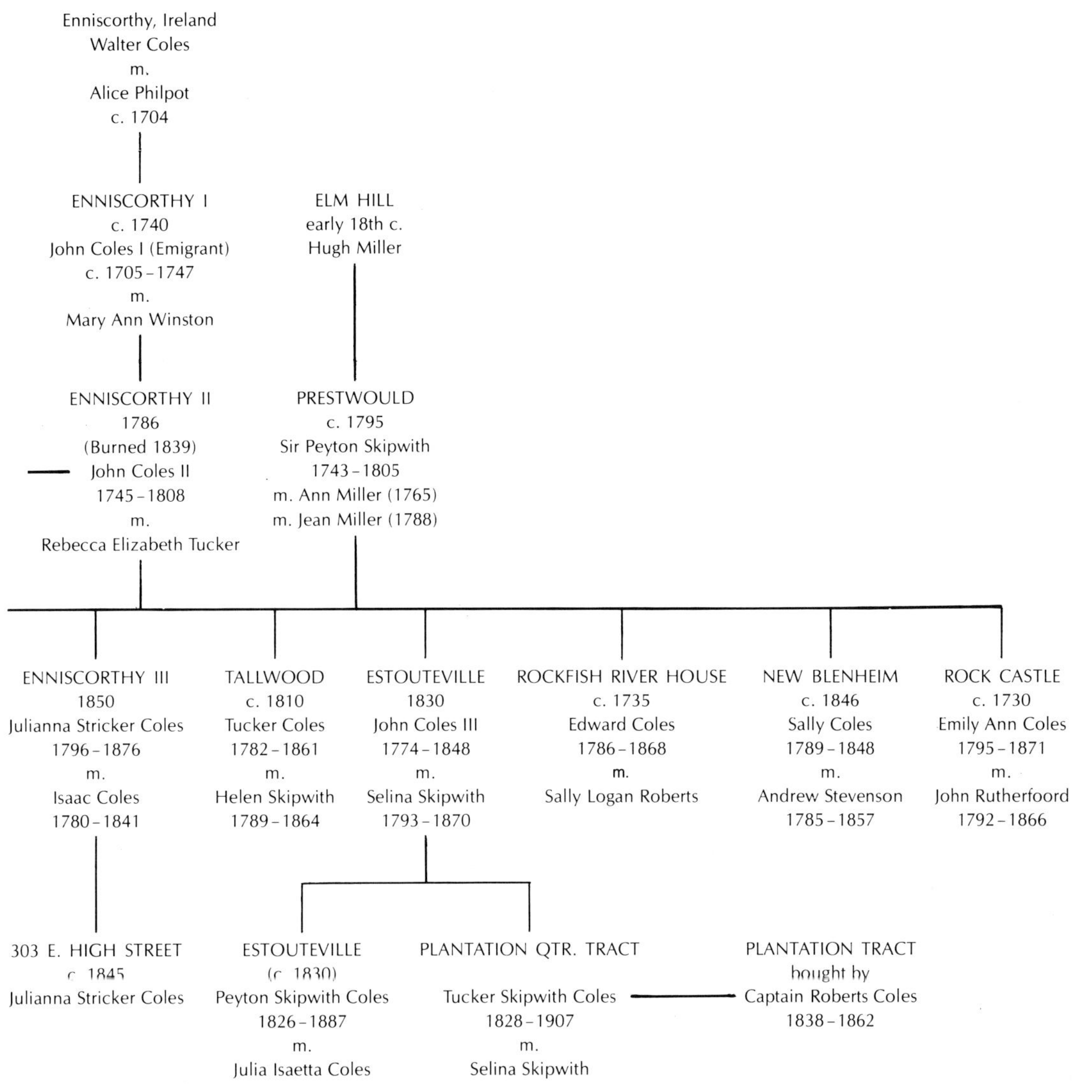

1.
Genealogy of houses, showing name of house, date of building, and name of builder. (K. Edward Lay.)

give some sense of life in the plantation house as it evolved over a little more than a century, from about 1740 to 1865.

Happily, we may catch this evolution as it appeared. By choosing a family of builders, we have availed ourselves of an exceptional view, through one family's papers, of the economic and social role played by a group of houses in the Piedmont landscape of Virginia over a given period of time. The questions addressed will be as specific in their field as are the measured drawings. How were the houses built, how financed? Under what economic stimulus? How did they function, how relate to the land, and to the social needs of their periods? In account books, tax lists, wills, and personal letters the answers to such questions may be found. We have, in fact, a close-up view of four generations of one family of antebellum Virginia. Here is a picture of the plantation society; of how they built their houses, how they lived, worked, and played; and indeed of how the houses themselves helped to shape the character of the people.

Architecturally the houses have been placed in their period, and presented through photographs, site plans, and measured drawings. Especially relevant to this county of Albemarle has been the influence of Thomas Jefferson. Through their houses we have been able to explore the relationship of this family to a whole society, from Mr. Jefferson on down through the social scale. We have the merchant-factor, Charles Irving; we have slaves; we have "the poor of the parish," and those workmen and artisans who sawed the timber, burnt the bricks, and turned a fine bit of cabinetwork. A house, we see, reflects all of this, and family life as well.

We accompany family members on shopping trips to the northern states, to the "painting room" of Thomas Sully. We have a look at the books in their libraries, and we sit down at their tables. Near the end of their story we follow Edward Coles as he frees his slaves, long before the war that freed them all. We see his son die fighting for the Confederacy. We see the curtain fall on the end of the Southern way of life. Only the houses have survived.

We show their advance, from the log pen to the simple, vernacular, story-and-a-half house to the fine Roman portico, moving on at last to the elegant Greek Revival. The columns, if one likes, held the wilderness at bay. Box-lined walks between flowering beds mediated between the house and the land. The houses we shall study stopped short of the romantic parks and vistas of the same period in England. Nevertheless they relate to the land. They do not stand alone.

As works of art they are not something isolated, created out of pattern books for all time. We see portraits, furniture, all reflecting change, and reflecting to no small extent the sort of houses their owners desired. We need to supplement our architectural study with a feeling for the environment, and for human and social change. It is in this sense that the work of all three authors contributes to the picture as a whole.

Our final pages will show which of the family houses have survived. They have lost, of course, their primary economic role, but in their timeless role of offering aesthetic pleasure and a civilized way of life, many of them, happily, remain with us today. Those that have vanished, or fallen victim to remodeling or neglect, are worth recalling both on their own account and because without them the family story, the steps in a progression, would be incomplete.

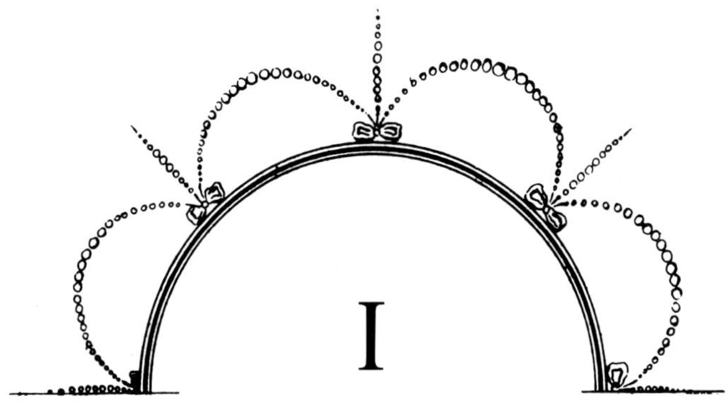

I

John I, c. 1705–47

The first of our family of houses was not actually a country house. It was the first house built on Church Hill in Richmond, William Byrd's newly laid-out city on the James. John Coles I (as we shall call him, because he was the first in a line of Johns) had come over from Enniscorthy, Ireland, to make his fortune as one of the merchants engaged in shipping tobacco. On May 28, 1741, we find him dining with William Byrd, perhaps in Coles's own new house.[1] It was just one block removed from the site of the new church, going up in this same year. For Coles it was a fitting as well as a splendid location. He had been a member of the vestry of the old Curles Church, and was to be a church warden and an active member of the new church designed to serve the city about to be raised at the falls of the James.

Actually, no site could have been more appropriate to a man engaged in trade. The soil of the coastal plain (or Tidewater), laid off in the great single-crop plantations, was wearing out. During this period, roughly between 1730 and 1750, planters were crossing the tide line, flocking in numbers into the new Piedmont country. Geologically the line was plainly marked; here, on a base of metamorphic rock, the continent rose abruptly from the unconsolidated sedimentary soil of the coastal plain. Socially and economically the tide line marked a similiar division. Younger sons, men making their own way and only occasionally favored with the large patents of an earlier day, were taking up the land above the falls. From his chosen house site, on a hill above the river, Coles could see the tobacco coming in from the upper country, to be placed aboard the ships waiting below the falls.

We should like to know more about such a man, coming to the new world without lands assured by patent and, so far as we know, having no established connection with the great mercantile firms of London and Glasgow. Neither was he a penniless or indentured youth; Coles's father was, in fact, a prosperous townsman. The town of Enniscorthy stands at the head of navigable water on the river Slaney; in the early eighteenth century it was a busy port. For nearly thirty years John's father, Walter Coles, was port reeve (equivalent to customs officer) of the town. Other members of the family appear regularly in the town records, including one Philip Coles, gent., who owned a malt house, importing barley and malt. There were Quakers involved in this trade, and if the young emigrant Coles carried any letters of introduction on his voyage to the new world, one could have been to the Winston family, active members of the Society of Friends in Hanover County north of the James.

We first hear of John in America in 1739, when he was appointed a "Processioner," that is, one appointed to walk the bounds of property lines—an important function in that era of opening up the land. He must have already been married at that date, for a few months later his eldest son, Walter, was born.[2] His bride was Mary Ann Winston, youngest daughter of Isaac Winston, a prominent member of the Cedar Creek Meeting. John himself was never converted—or "convinced," as the Friends put it. Obviously, he preferred the more worldly company of his own church.

Nor was he at this time a poor man. At the time of his dinner with Byrd, he had already bought nine lots in the newly laid-out city of Richmond, to which, as an investor of consequence, he now added six more.[3] He was also, at this time, a Commissioner of the Peace. In terms of business, we learn that he had bought 1,500 pounds worth of wheat for export and that he was having trouble in engaging shipping. No Coles letter book survives. This scrap of information, so indicative of the size of his business, comes from the *Journal of the Council of Virginia*, which, on April 29, 1741, rejected Coles's request that he be allowed to ship his wheat to Lisbon, because he was unable to find shipping to Great Britain. This petition was refused on the ground that "all ships carrying provisions out of the colony. . . . shall be carried to Great Britain." "Private interests," the council virtuously remarked, "must give way to the public good."[4] Coles's predicament may have been genuine; on the other hand he may simply have been one of those independent merchants then probing the possibility of the more profitable trade with Portugal. The mother country helped herself to a large share of his profits in the form of duties. In any case, we cannot doubt that his dealings were eminently successful.

We may well ask how the young man from Enniscorthy had accumulated so much so quickly. The answer would appear to be industry, shrewdness, and trading on commission. The risks were great, but the profits were commensurate. In return for his wheat, he imported English goods, necessaries of life in the colony. At the time of his early death in 1747, he had estimated the contents of his store to be worth the £800 cash left his daughters in his will. But goods and ready money play only a small part in this document, proved in the office of the clerk of Henrico County in the years 1747 and 1748. Like other successful men, Coles had put his mercantile profits into the fine agricultural land north and west of the Tidewater.

Contrary to the general impression, land in the colony was not open to just anyone who asked for it. A yeoman ancestor of Thomas Jefferson, unable to obtain a patent, had had to buy a small tract from William Byrd I. Such large landowners as Byrd and "King" Carter make present-day maneuvering seem mild indeed. Land was tightly held, and yet it offered almost the only way to invest surplus capital. John Coles bought his, and we will not be surprised to learn that he acquired some of the best tracts available.

Land and slaves went together. The land that Coles favored most seems to have been in Lunenburg County (now Halifax County) on the Staunton River. This plantation, added to by purchases in Brunswick County dating from 1740 to 1746,[5] was willed, along with fifteen slaves, to the eldest son, Walter. The acreage of that plantation has not been determined, but as five hundred acres were left to each of the two daughters, Sarah and Mary Coles, we may assume that the portion left to the eldest son would have been considerable. We know that in later years four separate plantations were carved out of the original estate. The youngest son, Isaac, also received land in this area. However, it is the Piedmont land, left to the second son, John II, with which we shall be concerned in this book of houses.

William Byrd's enthusiastic description in *A Journey to Eden* could have inspired the purchase of the Staunton River plantations, but it was John ("Secretary") Carter, made secretary of the colony through his father's virtually limitless influence, who told his friend Coles about the land at the mountains. Old "King" Carter had warned a friend: we must "find some other ways than tobacco to employ our people or else in a few years . . . become beggars."[6] "King" Carter's son John was one of the first to take up land in the Piedmont. In 1730 he patented a mountainous piece of land, then called Great (now Carter's) Mountain.[7] He believed that it contained iron ore. The belief turned out to be misplaced, but not before Carter had told Coles that there was iron in the upper country. Major Francis Eppes brought word that the mountains presented no obstacle to settlement; Eppes too was patenting land, on the creek named after him.[8] John I, never one to be left behind, bought three thousand acres from Eppes on the long beautiful ridge, the continuation of Carter's Mountain, known ever since as the Green Mountain, always the first to show green in the spring because of its magnificent stand of tulip poplar. This was the inheritance of John II, and the site of future Enniscorthy.

In the meantime the Winston clan had also been moving up-country, into Louisa County, following the course of the Quaker migration up the North Anna River and eventually into present Albemarle, at the foot of the Southwest Mountains.[9] This chain of mountains, or perhaps we might better call them foothills, lies just east of the Blue Ridge. Albemarle, then still the north end of Goochland County, is a part of the Piedmont. Carters, Coleses, and Jeffersons were in fact settling the frontier. No doubt at the urging of his Winston wife, Mary Ann, Coles also bought land on Fork Creek near its junction with the North Anna, and near the Fork Creek Meeting. His father-in-law had patented 1,200 acres in the area, and Coles, with his sharp eye, was probably not unaware that there were mining possibilities there as well. Col. Charles Chiswell, proprietor of Scotchtown Plantation, was operating a forge. Bars of pig iron have been found on this site in recent times. For whatever reason, Fork Creek became the Coles home plantation, left to "my dear wife during her life on conditions she pay my children as aforesaid for the use of the same if she should marry."[10] Mary Ann contested the will. She did in fact remarry. After all, she was only twenty-seven at the time of her husband's early death.

John I—no Quaker and more a merchant and townsman at heart than a planter—speaks of "my house on the Hill in Richmond town"[11] with more than ordinary pride. It must indeed have been a considerable house, more elegant, we may assume, than the plantation house at Fork Creek, and certainly more than any claim-house erected at his various other holdings. These, in all probability, would have been simple log cabins, the minimum requirement for securing a deed to the land granted by patent. Such a house will appear later in our history. Coles's conception of his house built above the new city went far beyond such primitive building.

William Byrd had dreamed it up, this city on the James: "Not only," he said, "did we build castles, but also cities in the air."[12] The more practical consideration was that "The lots will be granted in Fee Simple, on condition only of building a house in Three Years Time of 24 by 16 feet, fronting within 5 feet of the street."[13] The site of the city, of course, was the strategic one, at the head of navigable waters just below the falls. Byrd, even more than Carter, had seen the new direction that settlement was to take, and Coles was not far behind him.

It was Coles, in fact, who stood up in the Henrico County Council meeting in the spring of 1742 and proposed that the small collection of houses on a river should be incorporated as the city of Richmond.[14] He was Byrd's greatest single purchaser of lots. It is one thing to build a city in the air, quite another to start building on solid earth. Although John Coles is little remembered in Richmond today, his name should come directly after Byrd's as a founder of the city.

His own house was built, not on the river, but on a high ridge that overlooked the falls. It fronted south, and in this, as we shall see, he had set a Coles family precedent. We can imagine him standing on his porch, watching the tobacco-laden ships as they moved down the river below the falls. His was the first house on Church Hill and certainly remained for some time the largest; it was this house that was chosen by Benedict Arnold to serve as a barracks when that archtraitor occupied Richmond in 1781. Coles built other houses as well, some on and some below the hill.[15] The first vestry of the new church appointed him their church warden and building chairman. More than one item in "The Vestry Book of Henrico County, 1730–1773," mentions his activity along these lines, viz an entry for November 19, 1744: "Peter Randolph and John Coles, gent., are appointed to agree with the cheapest workmen they can, to undertake and Finish the Chappel to be built at Deep Run."[16] John I was the first in a long line of Coles family builders.

Unfortunately, we lack anything like a picture, or even an architectural description, of this first house on Church Hill. Along with "all the lots and Houses on the Hill where I live in Richmond town,"[17] this principal Coles home had been left to the youngest son, Isaac. At the time of his majority in 1769 Isaac was already established as a planter on his father's land in Halifax County. He was glad to sell his Richmond property to his father's old friend, Col. Richard Adams. For some reason, perhaps Coles's early death and the subsequent prominence of the Adams family, the name of Coles is little remembered on Church Hill. What descriptions we have of the scene as Coles knew it come from the period of Adams ownership and are concerned only with the situation, not with the house itself: "The most commanding and excellent situations about Richmond are, the seat of a Mr. Adams, on the summit of the hill which overlooks the town; and Belvidere, an elegant villa belonging to the late Colonel William Bird [*sic*], of Westover."[18]

As John Coles owned contiguous unimproved lots around his house site, we are not surprised to learn that great trees remained there until a much later day. The house, indeed, must have stood in a grove, with ample space to the east for the necessary garden area, a pattern that will be repeated with startling regularity in every subsequent Coles house.

It is interesting that we at least know the exact position of this long-vanished house, determined from the tax records quoted by Mary Wingfield Scott in her *Houses of Old Richmond*: "According to the land books from 1783 to 1788 the site of [the later house built by Adams on one of the Coles lots] was unimproved up to that time. The explanation lies, it may be, in the fact that the square immediately north of this one, bounded by Broad, Grace, Twenty-second, and Twenty-third streets, which was classed as improved property at that same period, was the site of Richard Adams's earlier home."[19] Good photographs remain of the second Adams house, and it was tempting indeed to have claimed it as the one built by Coles, but exhaustive research has proved Miss Scott correct in her assumption. No description of the Coles house remains, beyond our knowledge of the view, confirmed by Colonel Adams himself. During the great fresh (we would now say flood) in May of 1771, this gentleman stood upon the porch of the old house. He was astounded to see a flood of forty feet perpendicular "suddenly coming down the river."[20] Allowing for some exaggeration of the size of the catastrophe, obviously there was nothing to obstruct the view.

John I had laid the foundation of the family fortunes; his sons were to follow a quite different pattern. Not one of the five small children left at his death, three sons and two daughters, were to desire a town house, nor did any of them settle on the Fork Creek land. This may have gone in fee simple to their mother, who had, as we know, remarried. All three sons were well provided for; all were, in fact, members of the landed gentry. Walter and Isaac built on the Staunton River land left them by their father in Halifax County. It is John II, the greatest builder of them all, whom we must now follow into Albemarle. John II was to establish that prolific family within sight of the mountains: the Enniscorthy Coles. He was to build, indeed, more and finer houses than his father had done.

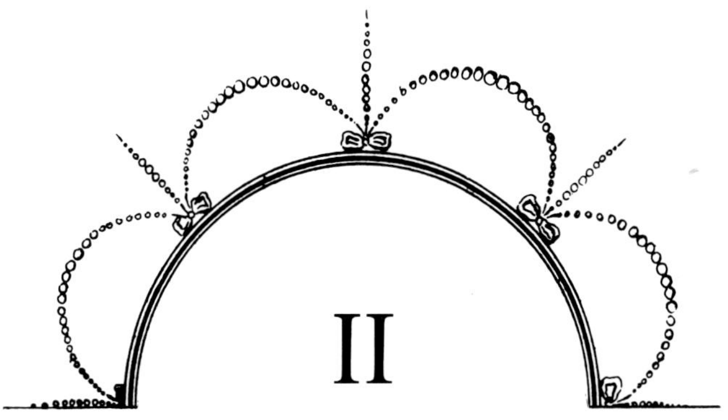

II

John II, 1745–1808

Enniscorthy! The name has the ring of filial piety. Even the names of slaves whom John Coles II inherited from his father echo the ties to the old world: St. John, Betty, Tabey, Sebrey, Richmond, Wexford, England, Phyllis, and Bristol. Such ties notwithstanding, this was a frontier land, a new world where John II was to find a livelihood, and to strike a new pattern of life. Without doubt some land had been cleared and outbuildings raised during his minority, as envisioned in his father's will. A road order as early as 1755[1] in the name of John Coles for a Green Mountain Road would show this sort of activity, although at the time our John was only ten years old. Still Enniscorthy could only have been a clearing in the wilderness. Taking possession of his land in the spring of the year 1766, the year of his majority, we can imagine young John riding through the untouched forest. The mountain was already green in that late April; the purple Judas trees and the white dogwood were coming into bloom. Beauty was there, and streams, and good deep red soil if one could make it out beneath the forest cover.

John I may have noticed the deep red clay—a sign, he had hoped, of iron deposits—but more important had been the sign of the forest itself. The poplars here grew to a tremendous height, raising their green canopy nearly two hundred feet above the traveler's head. John was about to make the most important choice of his life: where to fix the center of his domain. The Enniscorthy site was in general well chosen, but one may wonder why Coles placed his future home so near the deep hollow close behind the house. The answer, of course, is the spring flowing from this steep declivity. St. John de Crevecoeur describes it best:

> He [the settler] judges of the soil by the size and the appearance of the trees; next he judges of the goodness of the timber by that of the soil. The humble bush which delights in the shade, the wild ginseng, the spignet [a corruption of spikenard], the weeds on which he treads teach him all he wants to know. He observes the springs, the moisture of the earth, the range of the mountains, the course of the brooks.... He has formed his judgment as to his future buildings; their situation, future roads, cultivation, etc.[2]

As John II approached his new domain, he found only the barest beginning, a clearing in the wilderness. He too was a traveler, on his way to a future that he must already have determined should be on a large scale. Toward the end of this journey he was traveling on little more than a track through the forest trees. If he had come from Richmond, he would have taken the newly improved River Road, crossing the Rivanna at the well-named Mt. Misery Ford. He would have circled the horseshoe bend of the James where Scottsville now stands and approached by the "Irish Road," a name that now defies explanation, although appropriate enough for a man on his way to Enniscorthy. It was still wise to keep one's eye out for an Indian hunting party, shadows passing in the woods. He would have carried a gun on the bow of his saddle. In that virgin forest the bear and the mountain lion were at home. If he were lucky he might bring down the odd buffalo remaining from the herds that had once passed this way.

Any route would have been equally primitive. If he had left from the Fork Creek area, he could have come by the Old Mountain Road, the present route 640, and on to Secretary's Ford near Shadwell, joining there the famous Secretary's Road that Secretary Carter had built to connect the various quarters of his plantation in this area. (See fig. 2.) John would have passed the Jeffersons' home at Shadwell, and perhaps have backtracked a little to stop at Castle Hill, the one-and-a-half-story house built the year before by Dr. Thomas Walker, newly married to the wealthy widow Mrs. Nicholas Meriwether. He could have looked with some interest at this long frame house, not too different from familiar Scotchtown. He would have skirted Carter's Mountain and the site of the Secretary's Mill on the north fork of the Hardware River. He would now be approaching his own land. Col. John Fry's Viewmont lay just south of the stream. The back country, as it was called, was opening up; between 1732 and the Revolution twenty-one new counties were formed east of the Blue Ridge,[3] but distances between plantations were still great, and roads often impassable except by a bold man on a horse.

Colonel Fry was John's nearest neighbor. The old house at Viewmont burned in our own century, but when Coles passed that way in

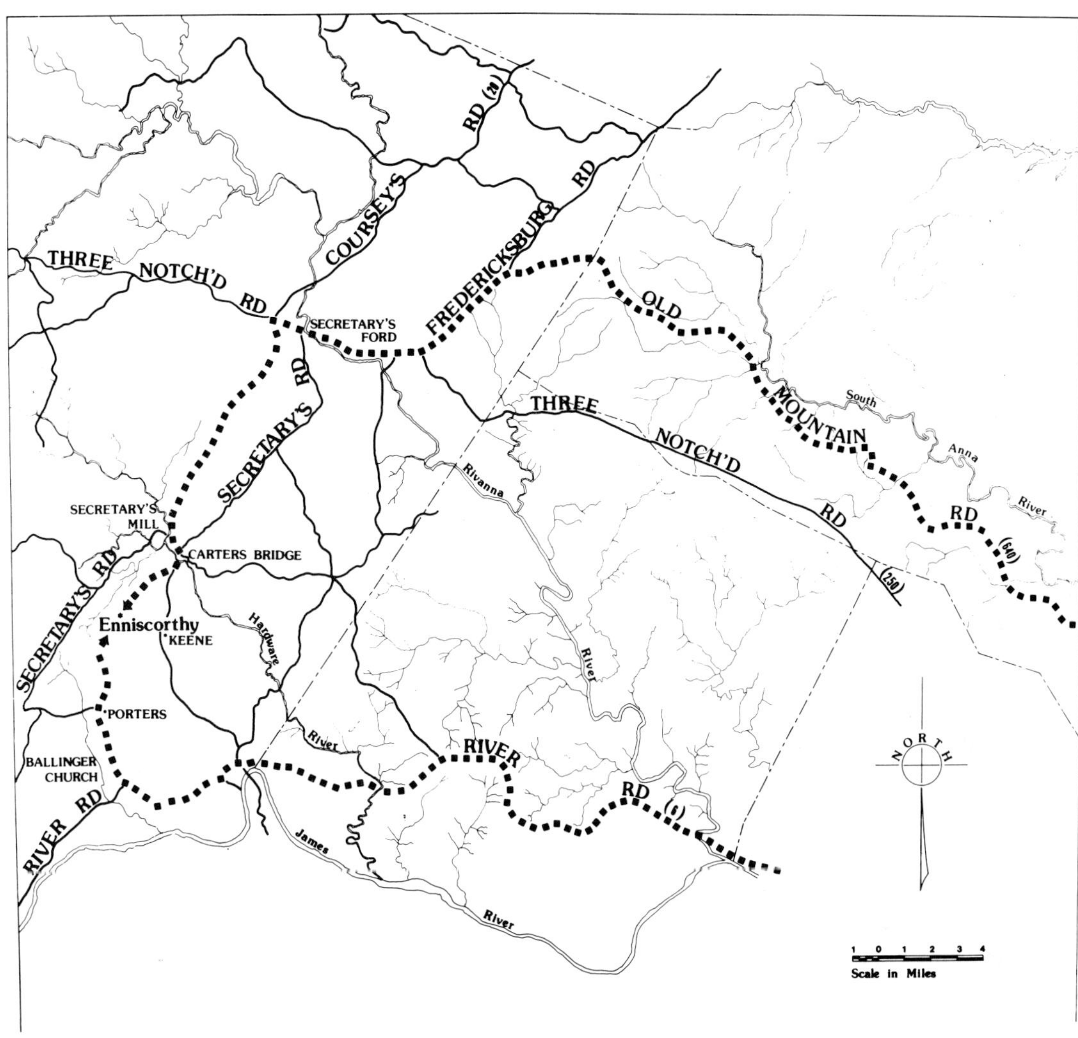

2.
Early road map, Albemarle County, c. 1747. The dashed lines illustrate alternate routes that could have been traveled by John Coles II on his way to take possession of his land on the Green Mountain in Albemarle. (From a 1982 map by K. Edward Lay based on a map in Nathaniel Mason Pawlett, Albemarle County Roads, 1725–1816 *[Charlottesville, Va.: Virginia Highway and Transportation Research Council, 1981], and a 1935 USGS topographical map; redrawn by Patricia A. Fiedler.)*

1766, it was a well-established home. John Fry's better known father, Joshua, had been dead a dozen years, buried on campaign in Maryland. His second-in-command, the young George Washington, had immortalized his chief by carving on that lonely tomb: "Here lies the Good, the Just and the Noble Fry." If John had stopped at Viewmont on his way up the mountain, Fry's son could have put him on the path to his new home. What sort of building he found there, and exactly where it stood, is difficult to prove beyond question today.

Family tradition identifies the house he found there with the frame Cabin in the Grove (fig. 3), which was recently dismantled and the log core removed to another site. This core may indeed have been the original house on the land, although circular saw marks on structural members and Greek Revival interior detail indicate a later period. There is reason to believe that it may have been extensively rebuilt at

3.
The Cabin in the Grove, photo taken c. 1920. Family tradition holds this to have been the first house built on Enniscorthy land, although all elements save that of the log core are clearly of a later date. (Photo by Edwin S. Roseberry, 1984).

this later time. If the log core actually was, as tradition claims, the first dwelling house, then Enniscorthy I was built on the ridge, close to John II's new house of 1784. It is this "new house" that we will refer to as Enniscorthy II, or, alternatively, as old Enniscorthy, to distinguish it from the present 1850 building.

Earlier houses—Shadwell, for example, and Viewmont—had been placed in relation to a river, or to the best available cropland. Like Jefferson, the Coles chose to build on top of a mountain. John II's house stood on the crest of a high ridge, facing a long view to the south and dropping off sharply to the north. When Count Castiglioni visited this new Coles house in 1786, he described the site with enthusiasm: "The situation, at the top of a hill, is such that the leaves fall later there, and appear earlier in the spring, than in the country adjacent. The calicanthus grows well, with such an exposure; the hill is called in the neighborhood the Green Hill, which, indeed, in situation and fertility may be compared with the foothills of Monte di Brianza. The mulberry and the vine should flourish here."[4]

4.
Tulip poplar grove at Enniscorthy, c. 1927. (Photo courtesy Mrs. Richard Holladay).

To clear the land the mighty trees must fall, but John spared the ridge. For generations after him the poplars were to raise their lofty heads on his green mountain. (See fig. 4.) We may think of them as standing in groves about the house, forerunners of the conscious landscaping of his son Isaac. His best cropland lay below him, to the west of the house; the land fell away toward Eppes Creek, opening up a view to the mountains beyond. If in fact the first Enniscorthy house stood on this same ridge, and we now believe that it did, the choice of a lofty site would have anteceded Jefferson's, giving the Coles first place in this new trend in landscaping—new at least in the American wilderness.

The question inevitably occurs, What sort of man was this young John, about to carve a new life out of the wilderness? What effect, in particular, did his father's early death have upon his upbringing? John

I had left funds to educate his sons at "the College" (William and Mary), but only Isaac took advantage of this opportunity. This perhaps accounts for the greater sophistication of the younger brother and for his public career,[5] something to which Enniscorthy John never aspired and which, in fact, he seems sedulously to have avoided. He was a planter, and one of the best in the state. It is our good fortune that he was also a builder. From the very first year, 1766, we can follow his career in that priceless, if strictly factual, record, the John Coles Account Book in the Alderman Library at the University of Virginia.

The first year's entry, 1766, shows "Col. John Fry—An item to cash wone [*sic*] at your house." John had ridden the four miles down Fry's path, so marked on the first Enniscorthy survey,[6] to play at cards with his neighbor at Viewmont, a pleasant custom that the account book shows was kept up during his bachelor years. More serious was the five pounds paid to Fry that first year "for a month's work of your sawyers." Card games notwithstanding, John had set to work at once. It is likely that some of the presently existing outbuildings were built at this time. It was a hard and lonely life for the beginning planter. The loneliness, at least, lasted for only three years. It came to an end on what was perhaps the most fortunate day in a fortunate life, February 9, 1769, the day that John married Rebecca Elizabeth Tucker (fig. 5).

He must have met her at the home of his older sister Mary, who was married to Henry Tucker and living in Norfolk. Rebecca was Henry's half sister. Such family connections led more often than not to eighteenth-century marriages, but we must give John credit for his choice. For many years Rebecca was to be the presiding spirit of that large and lively family, the Enniscorthy Coles.

Rebecca, a city girl, at first found life on the isolated plantation rather hard. When faced with the problem of making their eldest, little John, a vest, she wrote her mother: "Mr. Coles is very fond of John having a vest. I will be much obliged to you to get as much of stript cotton or chex as will make him one and make it for me and send it up by Dick. . . . I have a paper pattern. . . . but am such a dunce that I can't make one by it."[7]

She missed her John tremendously when he went with the Albemarle Militia to Williamsburg to frustrate any intention that Lord Dunmore may have had of raiding the arsenal there. John was no fiery patriot. He took a down-to-earth view. "His Lordship dare not attempt anything here for we have upwards of 1400 men who are in my opinion running the country to a very great expense when there is not the least occasion for half the number." He wrote this opinion to his wife on August 26, 1775. Four days later his mind is turned toward

5.
Rebecca Elizabeth Tucker Coles (Mrs. John Coles II), 1750–1826, of Enniscorthy, miniature, water color on ivory, by an unidentified artist, c. 1810. (Photo courtesy National Portrait Gallery.)

home: "I will get your thimble and my dear little Watt clothes [Walter, born 1772]. . . . pins and needles are not to be had here. I have sent a pistol by Mrs. ______, who set off to the Northward last Monday."[8] Was Becky nervous without him? What a pistol was doing among so much domesticity he does not say.

"Mr. Coles" and Rebecca both adored little Jack, who did not live long to enjoy his vest, or, indeed, to become John III. In that day of open hearths, little Jack's clothes caught fire, and before anything could be done, the child had been fatally burned. John and Rebecca chose a site on the ridge just southwest of the present house to bury their firstborn. It was the first bonding to the soil that John Coles called home, but far, as we shall see, from the last.

From very early on, John's plantation flourished, a business that required a number of highly developed skills. Tobacco, land, and slaves: this was the trinity, the form that wealth took in eighteenth-century Virginia. There was no other place to put one's profits. Even in

John II's time there were those who questioned the morality of the third item of the trinity: Jefferson, St. George Tucker, and John Payne, husband of John's cousin Mary Coles, were among those who suffered soul-searching doubts about slavery. Payne even acted upon principle. He sold his slaves and moved to Philadelphia with his family, including his daughter, the future first lady Dolley Madison. Of course Payne was a Quaker. There is no evidence that Coles saw slavery in any other light than as the given, the essential cog in his own economic place in life.

The plantation, in fact, was John's life, and tobacco was its staple. As well as planting tobacco, Enniscorthy went in for subsistence farming; the one-crop system was never carried to the extreme found in the Tidewater and in the plantations of the deep south. Nevertheless, tobacco was the money crop, and had to be gotten to the overseas market, which exercised such control over the plantation economy. The existence of a Coles Rolling Road mentioned in the Albemarle County Road Orders of 1791 and 1792 indicates that at least during the first years, slaves rolled the hogsheads of tobacco to a point on the James River, whence they could be floated on the flat-bottomed bateaux to the collection point at Westham. These early roads were the responsibility of the planters themselves, who "viewed"—that is, determined—the route of the roads serving their own property, the actual work to be done by hands also furnished by the planters. John Coles's name appears on many such road orders. An early one is mentioned by Thomas Jefferson in his Memorandum Book for July 5, 1769: "Have J. Coles appoint Overseer of Green Mountain Road."[9] The Green Mountain Road appears to have served as the Coles Rolling Road. It continued by way of the present Plain Dealing to the river at Scott's Ferry, where the name Warehouse Road on a plat of 1776 indicates the existence of a warehouse near Scott's Ferry at that date, and probably much earlier. John Coles's account book of 1774 records that he paid James Couch "By carrying down 47 hogsheads of tobacco from Drovers to Westham—£ 2–13."[10] In the following year a reference to a payment to Charles Irving for "waggoning" two hogsheads of tobacco would indicate that although the term *rolling road* survived, wagons often replaced the more tedious and labor-demanding method of "rolling" the crop to the river. (See fig. 6c.)

The method employed in moving the hogsheads was not quite as primitive as the term *rolling* suggests to the uninitiated. Actually, an axle was inserted in the hogshead, which was then drawn by oxen (fig. 6d). The roads were primitive enough. It was then loaded on a bateau (fig. 6b), an ingenious river craft of extremely shallow draft, capable of

6.
Transportation of tobacco. (a) *The double dugout canoe: fifty to sixty feet long, the invention of the Reverend Robert Rose to carry his crop from the Tye River area, far up-country, c. 1750. It could carry a load of from five to ten hogsheads of tobacco.* (b) *Bateau: wood, forty feet long, very shallow draft (c. four inches), capacity of up to eight hogsheads. This craft could negotiate all but the James River falls at Richmond; a canal was built at that point in 1784.* (c) *Wagons: two hogsheads.* (d) *Rolling in hoops, most often drawn by ox teams: hence the early expression* rolling road. *(Photo by Pauline Page, from William Tatham,* Essay on Tobacco Culture *[London, 1800].)*

carrying some eight hogsheads of tobacco. Inspection at the various warehouses was rigidly enforced by law, as was the size of the hogsheads "not to exceed 48" in the length of the stave, or 30" at the head."[11] Coles was sometimes paid in hard money; at other times, and perhaps more frequently, the value of his crop was used as credit in the customary system of barter.

Prices received at the warehouses varied from year to year and according to quality, but it is clear that Enniscorthy tobacco was profitable. In 1773 Coles sold three hogsheads at Warwick, a warehouse on the James below the falls, for £32.6.8. The value of tobacco relative to the cost of goods and services is rather hard to come by, due to the universal practice of barter, but we may note that imported goods were relatively high. In 1770 Coles paid £1.2.6 for a pound of tea! Luxuries, apart from those raised at home, were few and far between. Labor and even skilled local services were relatively cheap. By 1783, the year of Coles's first contract with the builder Frank Weathered,[12] 2,000 lbs. of tobacco, or the equivalent of £35, was sufficient to pay a large part of the cost of his new house.

The last year of the colonial period, 1774, is not a bad time to take a look at the domestic economy as practiced at Enniscorthy. By that year John's mother-in-law, the lady born Rebecca Elizabeth Travis in old Jamestown in 1727, had come to live with her daughter. She paid her own way, as so many widowed and single women did, through the hire of slaves in her possession; many of them accompanied her to her son-in-law's plantation. In that year Coles bought tea (Did it still cost more than a pound?), four bottles of snuff, and two yards of flannel on her behalf—comforts obtained from the merchant Charles Irving. Coles was clearly acting also as an agent for Irving at this date. He maintained credit at Irving's Howardsville store, and he passed on goods to his less affluent neighbors, in return for services rendered. For example, William Fortune and Shadrack Hitchcock both repaid Coles for goods such as "Sole leather for shoes [probably tanned by Coles himself], 2 handkerchiefs from Charles Irving, a bottle of Whiskey," with three or four days reaping in July 1774.[13]

There is no doubt that the role played by Coles as a distributor of goods, and also at times as a banker extending credit to his neighbors, was a service to the community, nor can we imagine that he lost by these exchanges. Time after time he paid for services with pork, corn, meal, and bacon; the more skilled craftsmen in his employ might also receive beef and bottles of brandy for their labor. Enniscorthy farm produced it all, including the brandy. He appears to have been on easy terms with his country neighbors; they were too near his own land and he was too dependent on their services to have assumed any of the superior airs occasionally seen among the Tidewater gentry.

Charles Irving, as the merchant and supplier for southside Albemarle, deserves special notice. He was an importer of English goods, a factor for the firm of Henderson McCaul in Glasgow. His store was in Howardsville, a town now virtually vanished from the scene, but once a busy river port. A surviving contract of October 1771 with the planter William Cabell, Jr., no doubt contains the same terms enjoyed by Coles.

> That I Charles Irving, as factor for Henderson McCaul & Co. merchants in Glasgow (Scotland) do oblige myself to furnish William Cabell, Jr. (from the store now kept by me in Albemarle County, Virginia) with all the goods which he the said Cabell shall have occasion of at 50% on their first cost, after making the proper allowance on all articles which have a Debenture, drawback, or bounty on exportation. And is further agreed by and between the parties that the balance due either party on the first day of September in every year shall carry interest from that time until paid.
>
> Witness my hand this 4th day of October, 1771.
>
> Charles Irving[14]

His dealings with Coles lasted from 1770 until Irving's death in 1794, only shaken by the coming of Revolution, and by the total depreciation of currency following that war. Coles supplied Irving with various farm products, but his major source of credit was tobacco. In 1775, the opening year of the Revolution, Irving refused to take Coles's crop; Coles noted in his account book that Irving "gave as a reason that the laws of my country prevented his sending it out of the country. I then sold the Tob^{o} to Thomas Pleasants of Henrico . . . I put the money in the Treasury . . . I have been obliged to pay the debt [to Irving] as stated above (in full) and can only draw the interest for the money put into the Treasury."[15] The affair was not settled for another five years after Irving's death in 1794, when Coles was at last forced to pay the debt. It was this same default by the treasury of the infant United States that caused Jefferson to complain that although he had sold a considerable piece of land before the war, he ultimately received in treasury notes only as much for his land as would buy a coat!

In spite of these difficulties Coles continued to deal with the merchant on the James, where the wide, slow river reached to the world of the Glasgow mills—and even to the world of culture, for Irving carried books.[16] Nothing remains of the old river port; even the later nineteenth-century buildings have fallen into disrepair, abandoned now, although a single modern frame shed stands upon old handhewn beams, supported by studs cut with straight saw marks.

We must not think of John Coles as an isolated up-country man, dependent on Irving for contact with the outside world. He was familiar with Williamsburg and the Tidewater. His good friends the Drummonds lived near the famous old house at Green Spring, the "wilderness palace" built by Governor Berkeley in the seventeenth century. A most interesting and indeed delightful letter of 1771 from Mrs. Drummond to Jefferson shows Coles engaged in a lively exchange of trees and plant material. In this matter he seems to have been the intermediary between Green Spring and Albemarle. Mrs. Drummond regrets that the season is so late

> that all the valuable fruite, and flower roots, cannot be medled with, and I can procure nothing worthy of the Acceptance of my Amiable friend, except four Apricot Trees, One Medler______, and some pumgranuts. I am promised but everything, of the flower roots in Octbr. all freinds that I've applied to, declairing the roots now, wou'd perish if dug Up, and spoil those, they were taken from. I was vext, and tho't my Self like the Hair, with many friends, but the fall will determine. I hope You've not only received some huderds, of Grafts, by Mr. Coles, of the choicest Englis fruite Green Spring afforded, but that you have grafted them too. He promist to take perticuler care of them, and You Sr. may depend their all, from the best English Trees."[17]

Mrs. Drummond's spelling was her own, but it must have been a pleasure to receive her letters.

It is clear that John, a man with his way to make in an untamed country, would have been most interested in the practical examples of agriculture as practiced at Green Spring. The formidable Berkeley had not only planted an orchard and a vineyard there, "he had made attempts at silk and rice culture, and grew hemp and tobacco."[18] This early interest in silk culture shows that Jefferson was not the first with his experiments on Mulberry Row, where he too had tried to cultivate the silkworm. John Coles, less experimental, contented himself with the cultivation of tobacco and hemp, and of course with his famous orchards. These were later a source of many of Monticello's trees.

After Jefferson's marriage to the "sensible and amiable" Martha Wayles Skelton in 1772, the Enniscorthy and Monticello families were on close visiting terms. During a visit in January 1774 there is an item in Jefferson's account book: "Mrs. Jefferson paid the Coles for washing a gown, 2/6." Also on this visit Martha Jefferson lost £11.3 at cards.[19] There was a considerable exchange of letters, often carried by Mrs. Jefferson's own hand when the letters were from the Drummonds in Williamsburg, or from John himself. Some time after Mrs. Jefferson's death someone, perhaps Jefferson, must have been asking for her letters to the Coles. According to a letter from Betsy Coles to her brothers "the last time I saw Mrs. Jefferson's letters, they were in Mama's cap drawer."[20] Their fate after leaving this depository is not known.

The revolution brought financial problems to more than Irving and Coles. A typical letter from Andrew Drummond gives the picture:

> That you intend, my good Sir to lay out the vile trash, which we call money—in Young Negroes is wisely determined, everybody's doing the same with us, and that there has been so many belonging to the absent Tories sold, yet people are dayle [*sic*] coming from all parts to purchase them at most enormous prices. . . . Then tis expected twill all [paper money] be wist off very soon, with a wet finger, by order of Congress. Lord help us______

He quotes prices: "Butter 12D[ollars] per lb., Coffee 20 D per lb., Ribbon 24 D per yd."

> Since I wrote this Congress has directed all our paper trash to be called in. One dollar allowed for forty.[21]

If anyone was cautious and handled his business well, it was our John. Besides slaves, he was steadily acquiring land. The original deed to the 3,000 acres (fig. 7a) bought from Eppes by John I had been lost, probably before John II had taken charge of his own affairs. It was not recorded until the Albemarle November Court in 1777. In 1771 John II obtained patents for four adjoining tracts totaling 1,455 acres.[22] Two more tracts of 200 acres each were bought from John Fortune and Richard Oglesby respectively. The Fortunes, incidently, were black. Contrary to the general impression in regard to such matters, William Fortune had received his land by patent. However, as we can see from John Coles's account book, the Fortunes failed to keep all of this original patent.

There was no way of stopping Coles. On one side he was expanding along Totier Creek and on the other along Eppes and Beaverdam creeks. 1780 saw an additional patent of 706 acres on Totier, contested by one John Wilkinson, who later settled out of court. In 1785 more land was bought on Beaverdam from the Melton family, near the grist mill that Coles was already operating on the Hardware River. In 1783 his holdings in Albemarle already totaled 5,000 acres. By 1807, the year before his death, Albemarle tax records show Coles's holdings to be 9,299 acres, making a grand total, including land in other counties, of 14,475 1/2 acres. (Fig. 7c shows only John II's contiguous tracts in Albemarle.)

At the same time that John Coles was expanding his holdings in land, he was taking his part in those public duties devolving upon a large landowner. In addition to being an officer in the Albemarle

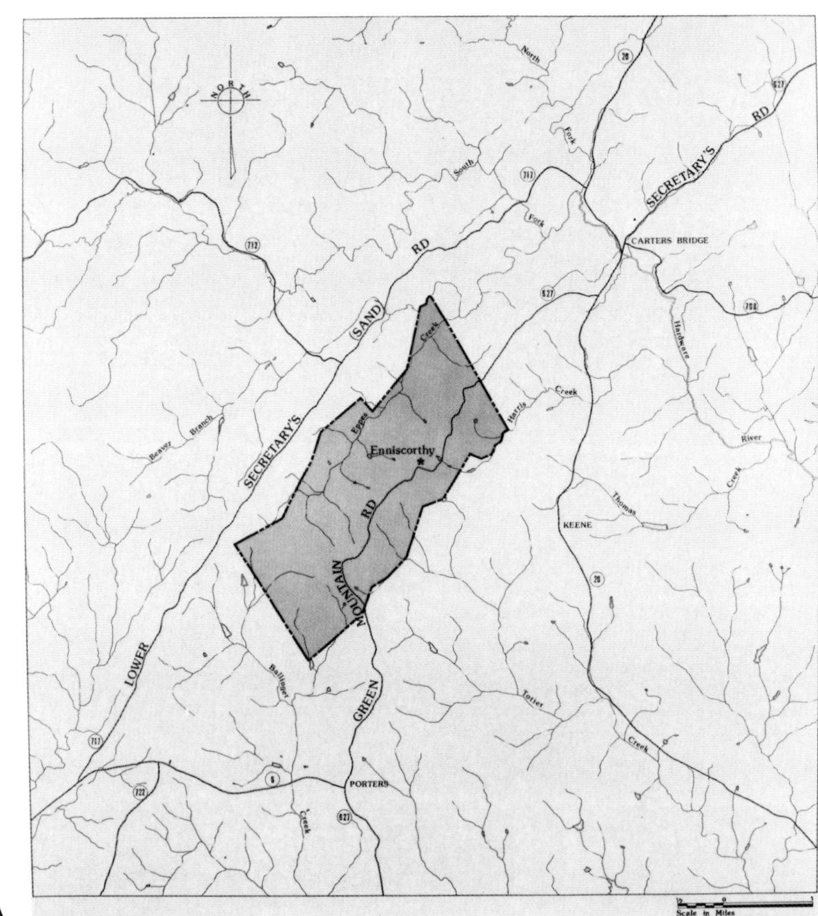

A

B

7.
Contiguous land holdings of Coles family in Albemarle County. (a) *Willed to John Coles II, 1747: 3,000 acres purchased by John I from heirs of Francis Eppes, c. 1740–47.* (b) *1776: John II, 4,750 acres.* (c) *1808: c. 7,000 contiguous acres in Albemarle at the time of John II's death. Total acreage acquired by John II, 14,475½ acres, including some 7,475 acres outside the home tracts.* (d) *1863: 11,500 acres, greatest extent of contiguous land holdings by descendants of John Coles II in Albemarle. (Drawings by Patricia A. Fiedler;* a, b, c *based on research by Cynthia Fink, Brian Katen, and Foster Paulette; under the supervision of William D. Rieley.) (These maps also appear in enlarged form on the front and back endpapers of the book.)*

NORTH
SECRETARY'S RD
Redlands
CARTERS BRIDGE
Edgemont
STAUNTON
(SAND)
RD
Viewmont
FORGE CHURCH
Calycanthus Hill
JAMES
SECRETARY'S
Enniscorthy
RIVER
Tallwood
RD
KEENE
PLAIN DEALING
TURNPIKE
Hampstead
MOUNTAIN
Woodville
LOWER
GREEN
DYERS MILL
PORTERS
Scale in Miles
C

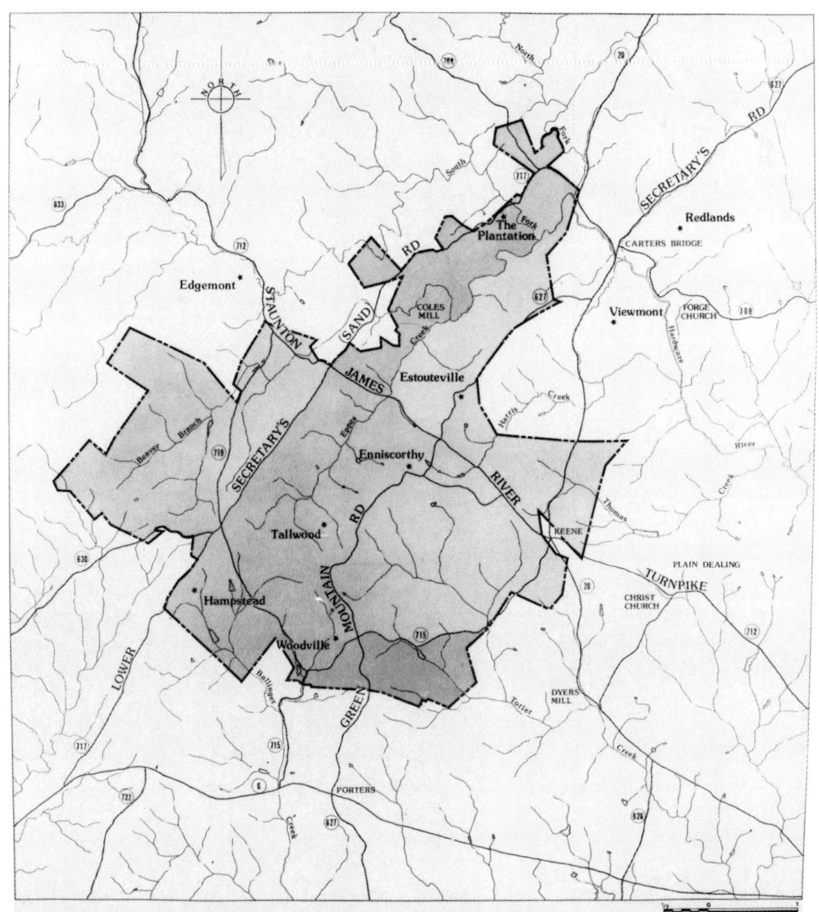
NORTH
SECRETARY'S RD
Redlands
CARTERS BRIDGE
The Plantation
Edgemont
STAUNTON
(SAND)
RD
COLES MILL
Viewmont
FORGE CHURCH
JAMES
Estouteville
SECRETARY'S
Enniscorthy
RIVER
Tallwood
RD
KEENE
PLAIN DEALING
TURNPIKE
CHRIST CHURCH
Hampstead
MOUNTAIN
Woodville
LOWER
GREEN
DYERS MILL
PORTERS
Scale in Miles
D

Militia (he resigned as county lieutenant in 1781), he served as Church Warden for the parish of St. Anne's. The parish at that time included all the territory north of the James from the town of Columbia to the Nelson County line, and as far to the north as a line from what is now Zion's Crossroads, through Charlottesville's Main Street, Ivy, and Greenwood, to Jarman's Gap. The inhabitants of this widely scattered area were all required to pay tithes for the support of the established church. The earliest surviving vestry book for St. Anne's (1771–84) shows Coles as church warden and most active vestryman for the whole period.

It was a tolerant time. Even before the Revolution not every man, not even every planter, was Episcopal, a member of the old established church. There was room in St. Anne's for the so-called dissenters, particularly for the numerous Presbyterians who had migrated down the Valley into Albemarle. When in 1776 "the dissenters from the Church of England and others in the Counties of Albemarle, Amherst and Buckingham" petitioned the Commonwealth of Virginia to relieve the dissenting congregations from paying tithes to the established church, John Coles's name led the list of those "others" who signed the petition for the relief of the dissenting brethren.[23] The name of a church warden at the head of this list of "others" is significant, for it shows the solidarity of a large landowner with his neighbors in a frontier county.

Not all these neighbors, of course, were doing as well as Coles. Otherwise he could not have acquired land as he did, for, as we know, he had no large original patent. The Meltons, for example, had fallen on hard times. Old Mr. Melton is listed in Coles's account book as receiving food, "a poor man of the parish,"[24] in 1775 and 1776. The son, John Melton, later served as overseer on the Rockfish farm acquired by Coles in 1782. The Melton land had been sold to Coles.

Such large acquisitions of land required additional slaves. The 1784 tax lists show Coles owning seventy-one Negroes. We may imagine the number of small cabins that were needed to house them. An insurance record of 1796 shows similar cabins at Monticello; they were twelve feet by fourteen feet, of wood, with a wooden chimney on one side, and an earthen floor. As a wooden chimney often caught on fire, it stood a little apart from the wall, so that it might be torn loose and the fire put out before the cabin too burned. No such record of an early cabin survives at Enniscorthy, but a servant's house in existence there until the 1940s is described as about sixteen by fourteen feet of logs covered with weatherboards on a stone foundation. It had two rooms, with a chimney in the middle, and was entered by two separate doors.[25] Even in 1809 a friendly visitor to Monticello had been somewhat shocked by the contrast between slave quarters and the mansion of the master.[26] We may be sure that Enniscorthy did no better by its slaves than did Thomas Jefferson.

Home industries, so encouraged at Monticello, were not as extensively practiced at Enniscorthy. Even weaving was farmed out; in 1782 it was done at Monticello. Coles bought his nails, usually by barter, from Jefferson's nailery. In 1804, nails were exchanged for eighty-eight feet of cherry plank. The beautiful parquet floor at Monticello was made from wood from Enniscorthy's trees. There was never any lack of material for barter. In 1783 there is an item: "Francis Wetherhead [of whom we shall hear more later] for 33 days work on my mill"[27]; in that year thirty-three barrels of flour were shipped down the river to Richmond. Besides the trade generated from Coles's mills, there were the two stills operated in later years. 385 gallons of brandy were produced in 1797. It was another source of trade and profit. Nor was Coles averse to experiment. In 1777, encouraged by Mr. Jefferson, Coles had bought a cotton gin, although as a matter of fact we hear no more of cotton in the account book. Hemp, on the other hand, continued to be produced.

Fine horses were a source of income as well as pleasure. John, although never a racing man himself, was a connoisseur and breeder of repute. From the early seventies neighbors sent their mares to be bred to his stud horses. There was Jupiter, who stood at Enniscorthy for a dozen years and was sold for $100 in 1810. Fearnaught stood at £2 for a season, a large fee at the time. Horse dealing would seem to have reached a peak with the sale of Mountaineer for £560 to Col. Edward Carter, who paid largely in slaves. With John it was a practical business; we cannot imagine him, like his brother Isaac of Halifax County, trading three city lots for a horse and a piece of fine linen.

Children had been coming as regularly as clockwork, an average of one every two years. Walter, John, Mary Elizabeth, Isaac, and Tucker were all alive and thriving in 1782. John and Rebecca began thinking of a larger house.

Building in the eighteenth century in Albemarle County was quite different from building today. There were no architects as such, only builders who were, at best, familiar with the English pattern books popular at the time. There is no reason to think that the Francis Wetherhead who had done "33 days work on my mill" had any exceptional training. The two builders with whom Jefferson was to work at a later date, James Dinsmore and John Nielson, had not yet arrived in the county. There had been no time to discuss architecture on the occasion the year before, when the Monticello family had paused some time at Enniscorthy during their flight from Tarleton's raiders, and now Jefferson was in deep mourning. His wife had died in September 1782; the widower was alone with his children on his mountain top. The Coles were on their own, without benefit, even had they wished it, of architectural advice from their distinguished friend and neighbor.

Typically, John was more concerned with adequate space than with style. In 1783 he contracted with Weatherhead to build him a frame house in the old style, now usually referred to as "vernacular." It was to be a dwelling house two stories high, built of wood and underpinned with brick, sixty by twenty feet, a single pile, I house: that is to say, one room deep. It was at this time that Coles recorded in his account book a "Bond on building my house, 2000 lbs of tobacco or £35."

Such a house obviously did not require much architectural sophistication on the part of either owner or builder, but for the owner at that time and place responsibility went beyond design. Plank must be sawed by hand from native wood of his own trees; brick must be baked—or burned, as the term went—from his own red Albemarle clay. Part of the great success and charm of these early houses was the blending of such native materials with the landscape in which they stood. John's house, as we know, was placed on a ridge that dropped away sharply behind the house, which faced south. To the west, one looked over Eppes Creek and cultivated fields to the Ragged Mountains, and beyond them to the Blue Ridge. Crops were planted along the creeks, and fruit trees on the slopes. The account book shows that sixty apple trees were planted in 1774, and the Coles Carnation Mayduke cherries were famous. We have no early record of the garden (perhaps because Rebecca did not keep accounts that have survived), but to the east of the house she must have already chosen the garden site that was to flourish through the years.

Although we lack an accurate plan, the garden was almost certainly laid out in the precise squares that were universal at the time. They would have been intersected by paths and probably bordered with close-trimmed box. In many of the old garden sites today the box has unfortunately overgrown the original pattern, but the pattern was clearly there. It has been said that this rectilinear ground plan persisted in America long after Europe had adopted the informal "English" gardens of the romantic era, because of the need felt for imposing order on a very real wilderness. Even when trees were used as part of the scheme, they were rigidly controlled, as Philip Miller makes clear in his *Gardener's Kalendar*: "such trees as grow too much out of order may

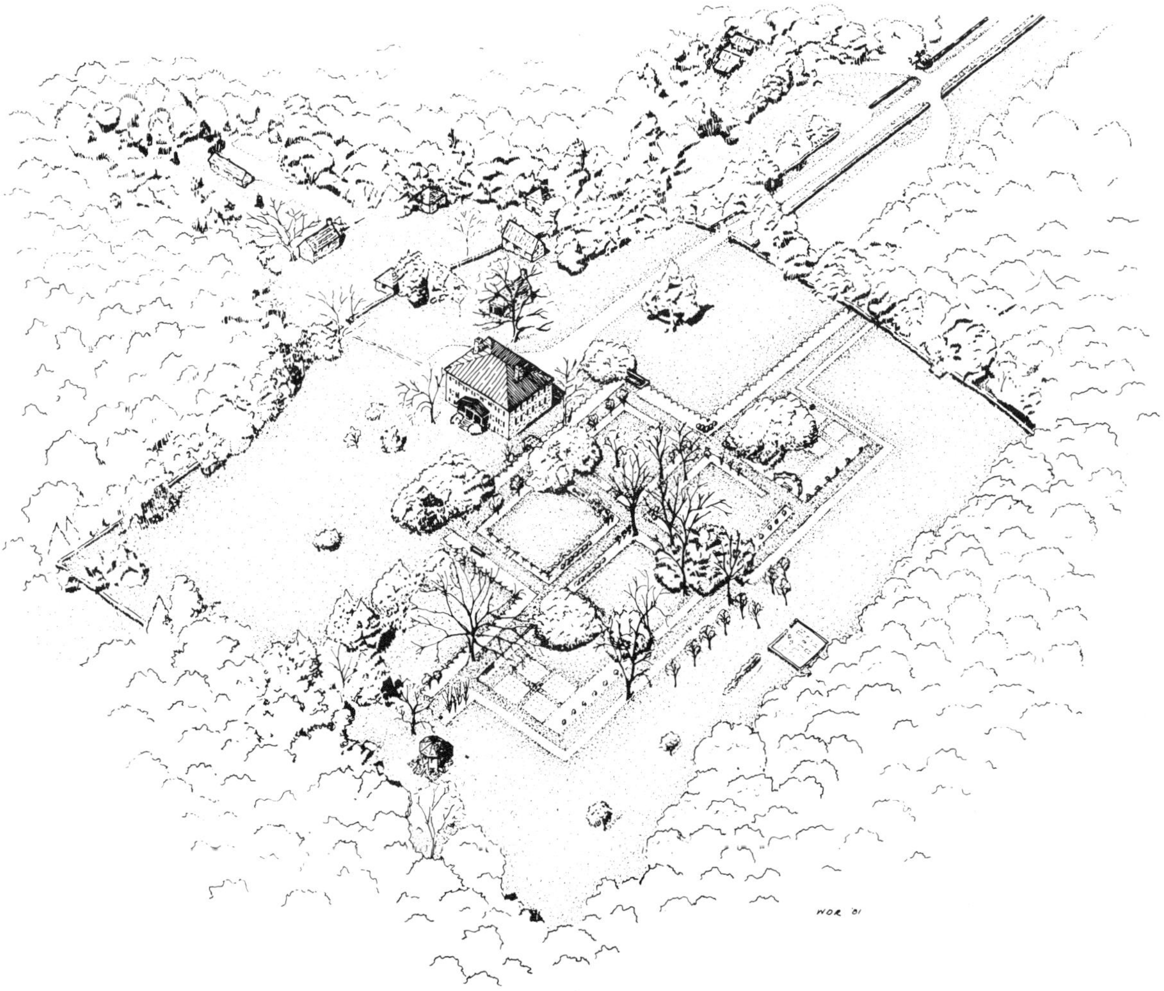

8.
Prestwould, 1792: site plan showing garden layout, 1808, as restored by the Garden Club of Virginia. (Rudy J. Favretti, landscape architect; drawn by William D. Rieley, 1981.)

be pruned, so as to render them beautiful; for this is a season [July], when wilderness and shady walks are chiefly frequented, so that they should be well kept, otherwise they will be disagreeable."[28]

Where was the American gardener who could argue with that? The lady of the house may have had to compete with the farm for the services of her garden help, but she had one strong point in her favor: flowers were only part of the garden scheme, for vegetables and medicinal herbs were grown there too. This was the serious part of the early gardens; for all that one ate, and the greater part of one's treatment when ill, came from these same formal squares. At Prestwould, the Skipwith home in Mecklenberg County, a model for later Coles gardens, fig trees and pecans bordered the wider paths (fig. 8). At all the Coles houses we find English yew trees, a distinguishing feature of their gardens like the Mayduke cherries of their orchards.

The planning and supervision of such gardens required both knowledge and constant care, and that was only the beginning of the care necessary to supply the table. As with all Virginia plantations, the working part of Enniscorthy was not under one roof; it was the plantation street. Here was the smokehouse, the kitchen, the icehouse, the dairy, perhaps the weavers' house, and most certainly the house servants' quarters. Typically this "street" consisted of a double file of outbuildings, usually including a schoolhouse, as at Tuckahoe, and later at John III's Estouteville. Indeed, the main house was the center of a small village rather than a single independent dwelling, a point often made by those European travelers who set down their impressions of plantation life. All these buildings contributed to the household economy; all needed to be checked daily, or as nearly daily as possible, by the mistress of the house. "Carrying the keys" was far more than a euphemism. Breakage and theft had to be guarded against. Martha Jefferson Randolph's rueful account of broken teacups at Monticello dealt with no unusual hazard, particularly to the beginning housekeeper.[29]

On the more positive side, it was the constant care accorded to anyone, black or white, who was ill on the place that really tested the skill of that busy plantation mistress. *The Planters and Mariners Medical Companion* (1807), by Dr. James Ewell, with its prescription for every sort of ailment, was available. It was one of the books from his mother-in-law's library at Prestwould later chosen by Tucker Coles. Among the medicinal herbs present in all Coles gardens would surely have been many of Dr. Ewell's prescriptions: rhubarb, powdered, was a mild cathartic; pinkroot (Carolina) was a vermifuge often in use, and Virginia snakeroot was a stimulant. Spirits of lavender, a cordial, could provide a needed lift to depressed spirits. The mistress, indeed, could find in her own garden remedies for most human ills. Doctors' visits were also noted as paid for in John II's account book, most often on the occasion of childbirth. Here too, both black and white mothers were attended. Of the twelve children born to Rebecca, only one died at birth. The account book for 1795 shows these brief entries: "Dr. Lochlan McLean by attendance on my wife—£ 1/14/12, and John Borden, by coffin for my son, -12- [shillings]."[30] That he also bought wine in this year for only the second time may have been for Becky's benefit. We may be sure that she had earned it.

Only a few of the old outbuildings remain at Enniscorthy, but originally there were many more. In fact, some have vanished in living memory—for example, the cabin referred to as Poky's House by one of her descendants. That Poky had Indian blood may be inferred by this corruption or diminutive of Pocahontas, and also by the appearance even today of her descendants. At Estouteville, the future home of John III, a slightly greater number of these necessary buildings survive, among them perhaps the most elegant of brick smokehouses.

Not only did one raise the ingredients needed for the table, one often had to invent the dishes in which they were used. Without a mother to help and advise her in the first years, the young Rebecca must have had a hard time. Perhaps she had Mrs. Glasse's cookbook to help her in the wilderness. If so she could have served this fine mushroom sauce.

To make Mushroom Sauce for White Fowls of all sorts. Take one pint of mushrooms, wash and pick them very clean and put them into a saucepan with a little salt, some nutmeg, a blade of mace, a pint of cream, and good piece of butter rolled in flour, boil all three together and keep stewing them, then pour your sauce into your dish, and garnish with lemon.

Mrs. Glasse[31]

With cream, fresh fruit, and brandy available at nearly every season, there was no lack of delicious deserts. The result was a savory, and no doubt better, diet than many enjoyed today. It was at the very least "natural." Gelatin did not come in a packet, it was made directly from the calf's foot!

For such housekeeping, time and many hands were needed, and both were in abundant supply. At the same time, living quarters could be very modest indeed. A house did not go up overnight. A second daughter and sixth child, Rebecca, was born in June of 1784, before John's second bond for £50.4 "payable when my house was raised and covered which became due December Albemarle Court Day 1784,"[32] was paid to Wethered. It was not until the end of 1785 that John Harris, bricklayer, had run up "my two chimneys as per agreement £11." In addition John paid Harris "By burning bricks £3–10, by underpinning my back porch £1, by 127 yards of seal at 3d per yard £2–12–1. By 235 side walls @ 4d a yard, £3–18–4, by your trouble in laying and cutting stones for my hearth £12—Total £22–13–3."[33]

There were also the finishing touches such as inside hardware, glass, hinges, and locks, which had to be imported. John's order went through one Henry Martin. Life in the first years had been austere. Now, at long last, John let himself go. Along with the hardware went an order for two mattresses at £8.4.6, three pieces of Irish linen, £9.15.10, and, luxury of luxuries, "By my chariott harness, £72–6–6. Import duties amounted to £13–7–7." Total spent on these luxury items: £130.18.4 sterling. Freight up the river, £4.13.9. Such an unprecedented need for hard money must have been paid for out of the return on twenty-one hogsheads of tobacco shipped that year and on the twenty-two hogsheads of 1786–87.

William Orr, who had worked for Jefferson at Monticello, furnished sixteen pairs of springs for windows, paid for in bacon and corn. Before the last bond was paid off in July of 1786, John bethought himself of a piazza, an addition once eloquently described by the painter John Singleton Copley, when building his own house in Boston. It was, in effect, simply a long verandah. "These Peazas [*sic*]," Copley wrote to his builder, "are so cool in summer and in winter break off the storms so much that I think I should not be able to like a house without."[34] This taste for a piazza shows the new concern with the native American climate. Just as the transplanted Englishman had taken some time to adapt his clothing to the American summer, so the design of his house had tended to ignore local conditions. John and Rebecca's piazza was not only adapted to the climate, it offered a closer link to the plantation street, the landscape, the garden, and the busy outdoor life that surrounded the house.

The last bond, "payable when my house is finished agreeable to our bargain entered into as per bond—£50" was paid in July 1786.[35] For this plain if satisfying house, additional furniture must now be bought. The cabinetmaker David Watson was boarded on the place for some of this work. This was the same Davy Watson who was the carriage maker at Monticello. Such workmen as Watson and Billy Orr moved from one plantation to another as their services were required. Their employers' account books show that they worked for Jefferson in 1781, 1782, and 1783 and for Coles in 1786. These two were obviously characters, deserters from the English army during the Revolution. What training they may have had before coming to Monticello is unknown, but it served them well enough to build an elegant phaeton to Jefferson's plan, and no doubt under his supervision.

The need at Enniscorthy was more basic. John II's accounts show a sideboard at £4. Watson then mended a table, easy chair, and looking glass, and went on to make a bedstead, £1.8. As his work at Enniscorthy kept him from going on to Colonel Carter's at Blenheim, John paid him six shillings extra. There followed a table 6 feet by 4 feet at £2.10, twelve chairs at £8, and two armchairs. Watson was paid in beef, pork, bacon, a bottle of rum, a bottle of brandy, a pound of wool, and eight days work of George. In addition he was given a credit at Samuel Dyer's store, called Plain Dealing, on the road

9.
Enniscorthy: walnut press made on the place, probably by local cabinetmaker David Watson, c. 1780. (Photo courtesy Museum of Early Southern Decorative Arts.)

between Enniscorthy and Scott's Ferry. That Orr and Watson enjoyed the liquor part of their earnings we know from Isaac's "Memoirs of a Monticello Slave": "Both [Davy Watson and Billy Orr] were workmen, both smoked pipes, and both drinkers. Drank whiskey; git drunk and sing; take a week at a time drinkin' and singin.' "[36] Which habit may account for the decline in Watson's wages during a second period of work at Monticello.

The George mentioned in the entry of 1786 was in all probability the same slave later referred to in Rebecca's will as "Carpenter George." The fine walnut press shown in figure 9 dates from this

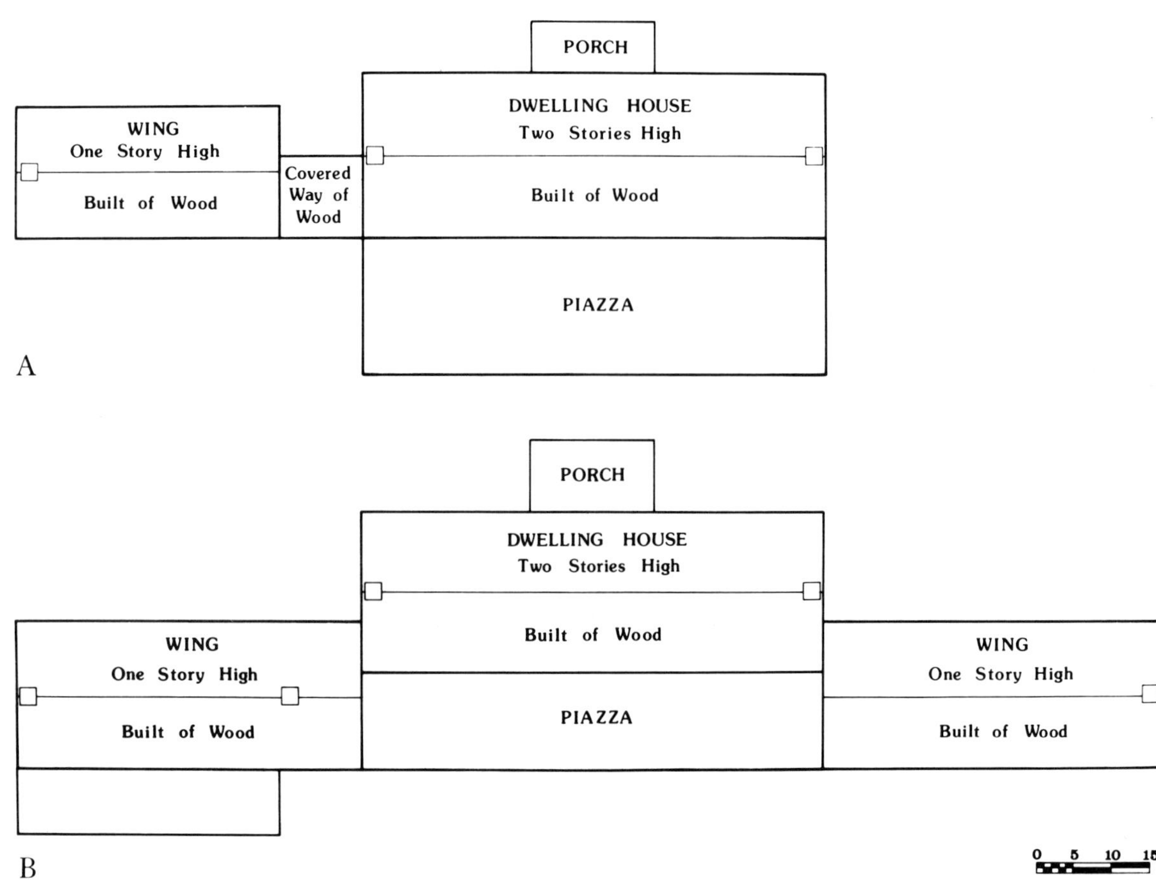

10.
Mutual Assurance Society plans of Enniscorthy House: (a) *May 20, 1799;* (b) *1810, dwelling valued at $5,000. (drawn by K. Edward Lay from Mutual Assurance Society Records, no. 351, vol. 13, reel 2, and no. 2274, vol. 45, reel 5, Virginia Historic Landmarks Commission, Richmond, Va.; redrawn by Patricia A. Fiedler, 1984).*

period; it traditionally was said to have been made by slaves on the place. It may actually have been the work of David Watson, with George's help. Liquor may indeed have caught up with this cheerful craftsman, but if he built the walnut press, he must have worked sober.

So was the second Enniscorthy neatly furnished. This vernacular I-form house was to expand considerably over the years; wings were added, and pinions, and again pinions—as small additional wings were called. The records of the Mutual Assurance Society (See fig. 10)[37] include diagrams of the additions existing when the house was insured in 1799 and 1810, a record of building as it occurred in John's lifetime. Later additions were the work of his son Isaac. It all culminated in a very impressive house, over 200 feet long, with a piazza probably not unlike that installed by George Washington on Mount Vernon in 1787. Unfortunately, this great house burned to the ground in 1839, and no record remains of the interior woodwork, but we may surely assume that it was as good if not better, as that to be seen

11.
Ornamental woodwork at Cragfont, Kentucky, by Frank Weatherred, the same craftsman who worked for John Coles II at Enniscorthy. (Photo by Helga Photo Studios.)

in surviving Coles houses. A later example of interior woodwork by Wethered gives some idea of what this same builder may have done at Enniscorthy. (See fig. 11.) Cabinetmaking and interior woodwork were done from English models and could stand comparison with the best of the period.

Glass and china, on the other hand, were still imported. Enough pieces remain (fig. 12) to suggest that the Coles did indeed purchase such luxury items during this period, or shortly thereafter. Secretaries also remain in the family. One of mahogany, with glass panes and a delicate inlay (fig. 13), was obviously made for a lady. No doubt it stood in Rebecca's sitting room, where she sometimes retired "from the family, visitors and bustle of the house, to spend in grave conversation a social hour over the little occurrances of the day."[38]

This quotation shows the lady and her family doctor enjoying a

12.
Eniscorthy: imported glass and silver ladle. The ladle is by Armistead Truslow, Lynchburg, c. 1820. (Private collection.)

private chat together; it is dated 1815, but the provision for privacy must have already existed at old Enniscorthy, certainly by the time of the additions made early in the century. Such easy, private talk had been virtually unknown in earlier houses, and was a mark of a new sophistication in a generation that previously had had little time or inclination for such refinements.

John, not himself over given to books, took care that the children should be educated, in the graces as well as in the serious affairs of life. In the year that saw the new house finished, there was an item to James Vaughan, dancing master "By teaching my sons and Polly to dance—£16."[39] The size of this sum indicates that they boarded with Vaughan. From 1789 to 1791 they went to school to William Rice, where it seemed that the favorite slave, Betty, went with them. One expense was buying Betty a "Hatt." The younger children were tutored at home, sometimes joined by the children of neighbors.

John was delighted when Patrick Henry spoke highly of the boys, after a visit to their cousins in Goochland. Fine boys, Henry called them. Isaac, Tucker, and Edward all went to college at William and Mary, graduating in 1798, 1803, and 1807 respectively. John was proud of his sons' learning, but expressed himself as being just as pleased that the girls "were not too learned."[40] At times he seems to

13.
Enniscorthy: mahogany secretary with inlay work, c. 1790. (Photo by Edwin S. Roseberry from a private collection.)

have had doubts about the boys too. In a letter to Isaac on the day after Christmas of 1796 he cites the woeful example "of your cousin Isaac, for what has he learnt [at college] after being at great expense but to play a good game of whist, and to talk nonsense . . . and gallanting the ladies?"[41] Heaven forbid that such a fate should overtake any son of his, but he is willing to give his Isaac the benefit of the doubt. He sent him more funds so that he would not find himself without money while at the college.

The two older boys had received no such fancy education. For them the first gifts had been of land and slaves. They had been set up virtually on reaching their majority as planters in their own right. Woodville, the next house that John II built on the Green Mountain, was for his eldest son, Walter, the first of four houses built in his lifetime for three sons and a daughter.

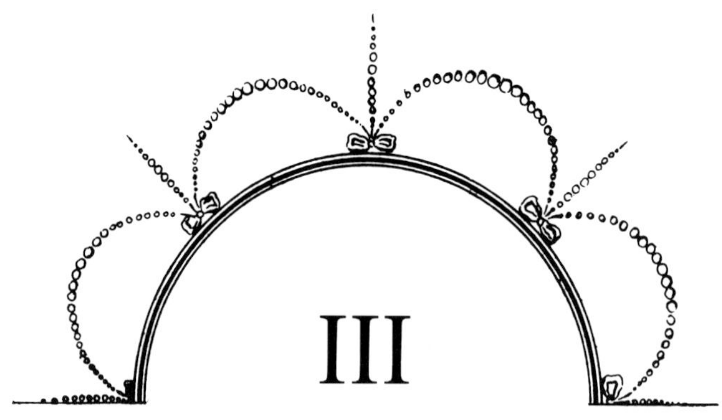

III

Some Portraits

The Enniscorthy family was a handsome one, as is abundantly clear from a look at their portraits. Unfortunately, we have no likeness of John II, or of John I, the emigrant. Rebecca, seen in a miniature still owned in the family, (see fig. 5), has fine features, delicately painted. Prolonged inquiry has failed to identify the artist who so skillfully executed the features and the delicate white cap and collar of his sitter. Not until the third generation was there a full flowering of the taste for portraiture.

Isaac was the first to sit for a now readily identifiable artist. He was serving at the time as private secretary to President Jefferson in Washington. He was in the midst of great affairs, ideally situated to observe the dramatic events of that summer of 1807. The president had sent him to Richmond with documents related to the upcoming trial for treason of Aaron Burr. Jefferson was counting on General Wilkinson, who had been his commander in New Orleans, as his principal witness in the attempt to indict Burr for his plan to take over that city. Unfortunately, the general's reputation was even then dubious; it was to come out later that at some time before the trial he had been in the pay of Spain. However at the time of the trial Jefferson was desperate for information from New Orleans. A letter of Isaac's in July to his friend Joseph C. Cabell quotes the president relieving his anxiety in a somewhat unguarded conversation with Coles:

"I wish," said he, "that your friend Cabell would consent to go to Orleans. . . . There is the deuce to pay there. . . . Claiborne has left Orleans and gone, God knows where, to fight a duel with Clarke, and if he falls there will be no one to represent the Government. I wish Monroe was here, I think I could prevail on him to accept this office, though he has hitherto refused it—he would now be of infinite value to us there." After a pause of some moments he continued—"If Cabell would go, and Monroe should still refuse, I will make him governor."[1]

This is a rare view of Jefferson, as it were, in undress, one that never appears in his own writing. For this we are indebted to the indiscretion of his secretary. We only wish that he had been indiscreet more often! Many of Isaac's letters to Cabell suggest that the president used him deliberately when he wished to launch a trial balloon. Isaac's diary is discretion itself: we learn only that July was intolerably hot and that General Wilkinson dined twice at the president's house. Meriwether Lewis, in town with the Indian chiefs he had brought with him to the capital, also is listed twice as a guest and appears as Isaac's familiar companion. Washington Irving was another visitor. "Your young friend Irving," Isaac wrote to Cabell, "called on me, and I had the pleasure of introducing him to the President."[2] Washington Irving, it seems, had not yet acquired his reputation; *Sleepy Hollow* was still in the future. Despite all this social activity, "Writing for the President" is the diary's most frequent entry. It was with papers relative to the Burr trial that Isaac set off for Richmond on the first of August, arriving for dinner on the third.

It did not take much enterprise on Isaac's part to repair to the studio of Saint-Mémin, recently set up at Mrs. Harris's lodging house to catch the notables attending the Burr trial. Wilkinson had sat, and so had Meriwether Lewis and his Indians. Isaac's entry for August 4 is laconic, as usual. "Dined with Mr. Hay [government counsel in the Burr trial]. Sat to St. Memmon [*sic*]." Jefferson, of course, had set the example; he had sat twice for the French émigré aristocrat Charles B. J. Fevret de Saint-Mémin (1770–1852). Saint-Mémin had lost his estate in the French Revolution and had taken refuge in America. He turned to portraiture less as an art than as a way—hardly, he felt, appropriate to a gentleman of his quality—of making a living. Following the mechanical bent of the day, he employed a Physiognotrace. The following description is from a work by Fillmore Norfleet.

> [This] unwieldy instrument consisted of a rectangular frame that slid up and down between two tall upright pieces of wood to which were attached a moveable magnifying glass and a projecting arm holding a pencil. With the eyepiece adjusted, the operator moved his head so that the intersection of the threads cut on the glass followed around the sitter's profile, the pencil all the while tracing the life size profile on a sheet of, ordinarily, buff-colored paper. Afterwards St. Memin finished free-hand the features and costume in black crayon which was heightened with white, and gave the finished product an opaque wash of varying shades of pink. The large profile he then reduced by

> the aid of the pantograph or tracer—long known as a stork's beak or monkey—within a circle on a copperplate, . . . the diameter of which was generally about two inches. After perfecting the outline, he worked up the details with a graver, and afterwards used a roulette—a tool made by a machine of his own invention—to finish the shading.
>
> When the crayon was finished, he placed the pink profile in a gold frame edged with lamb's tongue molding that held a glass bordered with a wash that was at times dark maroon, at others black, and always octagonal in shape. Frequently the triangular corners were embellished with a fanciful design in gold that varied, apparently, as frequently as his field of operation.[3]

The advantage to the sitter was obvious: as in modern photography, one could have a "true" likeness, and as many copies as desired. Also, and not least, the price was right: twenty-five dollars for a large likeness and twelve dollars for small engravings, including the plate.[4] For Saint-Mémin himself this scientific paraphernalia may have permitted him to avoid the self-image of "artist," still at that time a lowly trade. Surprisingly enough, the results were extremely attractive. Saint-Mémin, in fact, became an artist *malgré lui.*

Isaac certainly was pleased with his portrait (fig. 14a), for in the following year brother John had his likeness taken by the same artist (fig. 14b). Existing engravings show a right profile, lively and almost boyish in effect, although at the time John was thirty-four years old. The engraving, in fact, is more flattering than the original drawing. Both drawings and several engravings are still in the Coles family.

The next Coles venture into portraiture again owed something to their celebrated neighbor at Monticello. Ever alert to order sculptured busts of his heroes, Jefferson had collected a number by the brilliant French sculptor Houdon. When the less important artist William J. Coffee arrived in New York from England in 1817, he promptly contacted this Virginian patron of the arts. It occurred to Jefferson that the time had come for family portrait busts. Although Coffee's work appears to be little known today, he was an exceptionally able portraitist, producing elegant half life-sized busts in terra cotta that caught the personality of his sitters to an extraordinary degree. Jefferson was delighted with Coffee's work at Monticello and recommended him both to Madison and to his friends at Enniscorthy. "He gives less trouble," Jefferson assured them, "than any artist painter or sculptor I ever submitted myself to."[5]

Coffee spent most of the summer of 1818 working in Albemarle, doing busts of Jefferson himself and of his daughter Martha and numbers of his grandchildren. Of these busts, only those of granddaughters Ann Cary Bankhead and Cornelia survive today. Both are

14.
Engravings by Saint-Mémin: (a) *Isaac A. Coles, 1807;* (b) *John Coles III, 1808. (Photos, Pauline Page and National Portrait Gallery; from a private collection.)*

A

B

15.
Portrait busts by William J. Coffee, 1818: (a) *Col. Isaac A. Coles in uniform, War of 1812, terra cotta;* (b) *John Coles III, terra cotta;* (c) *Walter Coles, white plaster;* (d) *Rebecca Elizabeth Tucker Coles (Mrs. John Coles II), white plaster. (Photos courtesy Museum of Early Southern Decorative Arts.)*

now at Monticello. Three were done at Montpelier, of Madison, his wife, Dolley, and his stepson, Payne Todd. None of these survive. The Coffee bust of Madison is listed as bought by Edward Coles in the sale at Monticello after Jefferson's death, but it too has vanished. The Enniscorthy busts fared better, for no less than seven remain in the hands of their present-day descendants, three of the originals in terra cotta and four cast in plaster. We have Isaac in his colonel's uniform of 1812 (fig. 15a), John (fig. 15b), Walter (fig. 15c), the old lady Rebecca (fig. 15d) now nearing seventy, and a young lady who would appear to be one of the two younger daughters, either Betsy or Emily Ann (by then Mrs. John Rutherfoord). Betsy seems to be the best guess. Busts of Rebecca and John survive both in plaster and in terra cotta originals.

Each portrait head is a vivid likeness. Even in terra cotta, Isaac's eyes twinkle, his smile appears as irresistible as it was reputed to have been

C

D

in life. Old Rebecca is no longer beautiful, but she is alive with good feeling. There is a French delicacy—for this art, after all, was practiced most frequently in France—and an American straightforwardness in the presentation of the little figures, which are about 13 inches high and 8 or 9 inches wide. The busts were done from life on the site and were transported to Coffee's studio in New York. Rauschenberg's description of the complete process is of considerable interest.

Coffee then took the bisque busts to his studio . . . where they were fired to around 800 degrees F. The transportation of unfired or "leather-hard" terra cotta was made easy by the fineness of the clay used. Coffee probably brought his own clay in powder form to Virginia. Mixing the clay to his desired consistency, he would then cut away clay to form the bust. When complete it would be removed from the stand or platform, the base finished and freed of excess clay. The column would be hollowed to allow moisture to escape, thus reducing the chance of cracking during firing. The bust would then be air dried and packed for shipment to New York via Richmond.

In his New York Studio Coffee would make a mold of plaster of paris around the lightly oiled unfired terra cotta bust. Plaster busts were then cast from the mold. A comparison made between the terra cotta and plaster busts of the same subjects revealed that the terra cotta measured only one-fourth inch smaller than the plaster examples.[6]

Jefferson's account book shows that the terra cotta original cost thirty-five dollars, and the plaster busts five dollars each. They were just the thing for those who could not afford a Gilbert Stuart. The busts could adorn a mantelpiece, and the Saint-Mémin drawings gave a look of substance to the walls. It was the beginning of the Coles addiction to portraiture, so typical of this individualistic age.

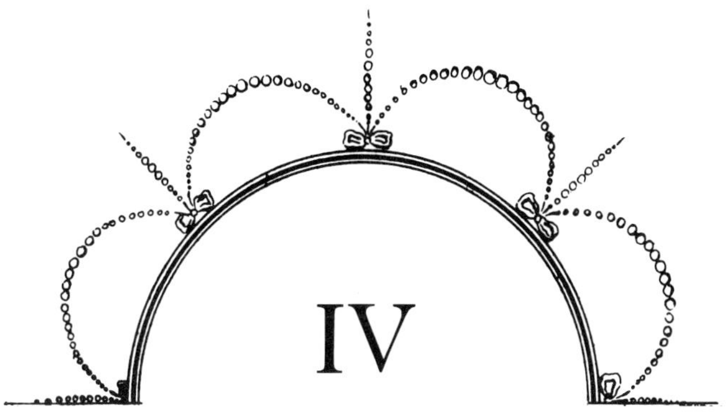

IV

Four Houses: Woodville, Enniscorthy II, Redlands, Calycanthus Hill

WOODVILLE

Coffee's gift for interpreting character is well shown in his bust of Walter. The young man is handsome, but lacks something of the imaginative flair of his brothers. Walter, generous and kindly, was content with his farm, his horses (of which, like his father, he had many), and his numerous family. He had served in the War of 1812 as a second lieutenant of cavalry at age forty, and was ever after a staunch supporter of Andy Jackson, for reasons perhaps more military than political. Much to the delight of his peripatetic brothers and sisters, this stay-at-home brother ventured from home on a trip to Washington, to attend the inauguration of his hero. Never one to question established institutions, he did not question slavery, but his will, probated in 1854, shows a sensitive care for the welfare of old servants. "It is my wish that my old and faithful servant Sally Carr, Fanny and Peter shall have the selection of their masters among my children. . . . There are among my slaves six or eight who from age and infirmity may be considered worthless. These slaves I desire shall be apportioned among my children herein named except my daughter Jane F. Fisher who I do not wish to be charged with any of them."[1]

When the time came to give Walter land and a house, John turned in the Ballenger's (or Ballinger) Creek–Warren direction, south toward Totier Creek rather than northeast toward the Hardware River. As recorded in the Road Order Book of Albemarle County, October 14, 1791, John Coles petitioned that a road be "viewed" from Melton's Ford to Tuley's Hill. This road appears to have run from the ford on

16.
Woodville, home of Walter Coles. The central section was completed in 1796 and the north wing was added in 1832. (Early-twentieth-century photo, courtesy Elizabeth Langhorne.)

the Hardware at Edgemont[2] to the vicinity of Porter's, and from thence to Warren along "Col. Coles's Church Road." This order clearly relates to the road from the Valley, for it states: "That this way will be much nearer to Nicholas's Warehouse [at Warren on the James] than the present road and convenient to a considerable part of the people of this county and also to a considerable part of the inhabitants of Amherst and Augusta."[3]

On a plateau south of the Green Mountain between Totier and Ballenger's creeks John began to build his son Walter a house. Woodville it was called (fig. 16). A survey of 1776 shows "the church path" leaving Coles's land in the direction of Porters at about this point. When John petitioned for an improved road, he may have been thinking in large terms of connecting the Shenandoah Valley with the James; on the other hand he may have been thinking of the family driving through the woods to church. In any case the new house that he was planning for Walter would benefit from this direct route to Warren and the river, for at that time Warren rivaled Scotts Ferry as a shipping point for tobacco.

The "Church" referred to in these road orders was not then the present one at nearby Glendower, but an earlier one on Ballenger's

Creek. The vestry book of St. Anne's Parish for 1771–84 shows that John Coles was church warden (senior warden) during the whole of this period.[4] His own account book bears entries related to payments "for preaching at Ballenger's Creek Church,"[5] and for support of the poor of the parish even after St. Anne's had ceased officially to exist. In 1782, a year of financial difficulties following the end of war, St. Anne's vestry and their rector parted company over the amount and kind of his salary. St. Anne's died, not to be officially reborn for another fifty years. Old Ballenger's Creek Church and the Forge Church near Carter's Bridge had both vanished by the time that John's son, John III, led the reorganization and the raising of a new church, the perfect little brick building of 1832, which is the present Christ Church, Glendower (See fig. 59). Here southside Albemarle Episcopalians still worship: Carters, Coles, Moons—members of the old families and many others gather on Sunday beneath the pines.

In 1794 John was still paying for the services of an occasional visiting preacher—one who would, in fact, perform perhaps long overdue marriages, confirmations, and baptisms—but most of his attention and expenditure was now on the new house being built for Walter. The owner in 1792 of 6,418 acres in Albemarle valued at £6853,[6] he was well able to afford this paternal gesture. Virginia custom no longer followed the English law of primogeniture;[7] elder sons were usually set up on their own when reaching their majority. As in the Coles family it was often a younger son who inherited the family house and the home plantation.

The account book entries for 1794 through 1796 show a number of building-related expenditures: to John Fortune (a neighbor from whom John had previously acquired land) £6.5.6 for sawing 2,900 feet of plank. This was presumably for the new house, or possibly for the wing added to his own house sometime prior to 1799. William Walker sawed another 1,714 feet. Cockwood, a stonemason, was engaged, and later paid for stone work, 60 perch, £7–10. The account with William Bates, the builder, is recorded in the account book.

1794		
May	William Bates for building house for Walter: By cash to be advanced to buy provisions to build a house, it being ⅓ of the price of the house he had bound himself to build for me.	£40
	By building a house for Walter to be paid when finished agreeable to the plan as per Bond annexed.	120

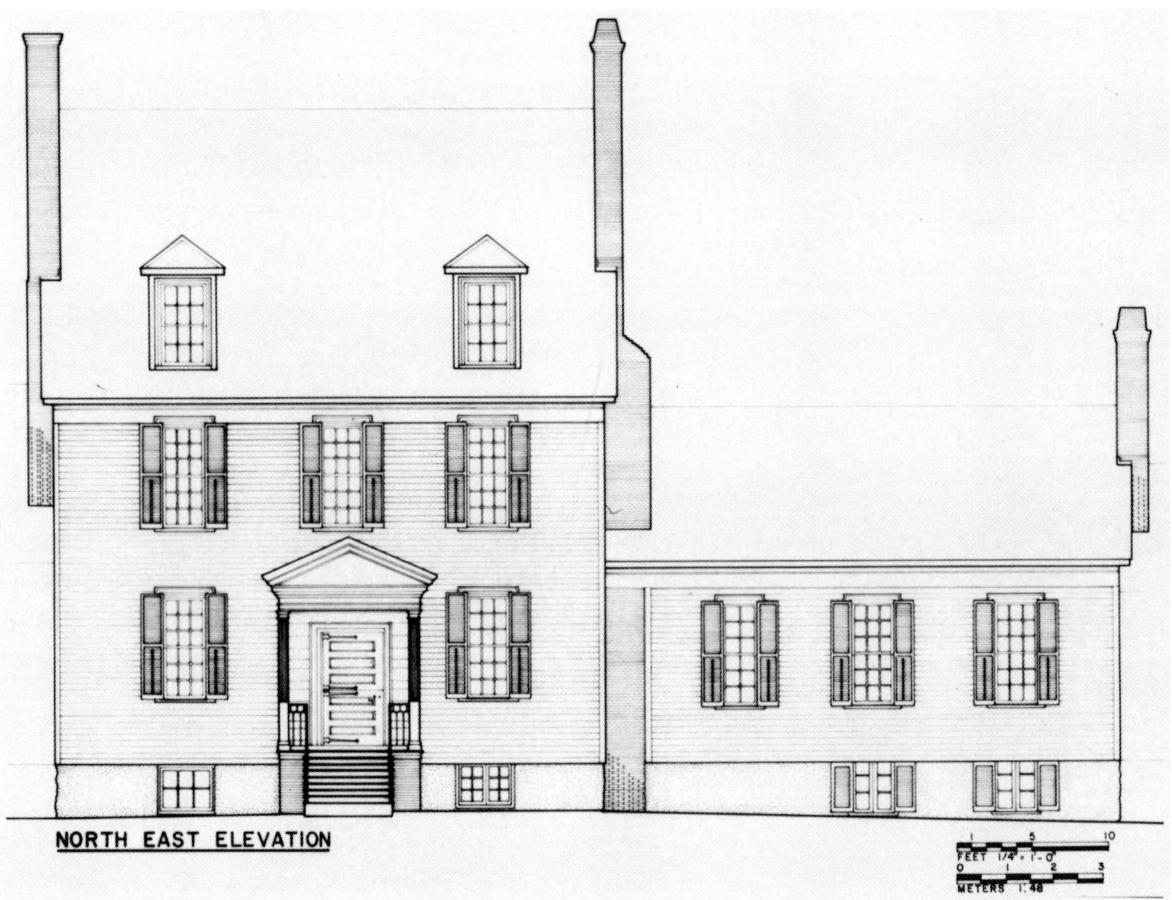

17.
Woodville, measured drawings: (a) *northeast front elevation;* (b) *first-floor plan. (Drawn by Thomas Dolan, 1983, under the direction of K. Edward Lay.)*

1794	By yr. fellow Toms hire from 27th of May to	
May 27	1st of December 1794 @ 20/ per month.	6
	By 12 thousand shingles at 13/	7.16
	By building two porches	18
	By 15 window shutters @ 10/	7.10
July	By settlement for additional work done on	
	my houses	29.1.10
		£228.7.10

1796		
Nov 3	By my note on demand	11.18.4
Nov 13	By Samuel Dyer	1.5
	By William Watkins	1.16
		£14.19.4[8]

Although the account is thus kept in pounds, shillings, and pence, it was actually paid for mainly by goods in kind. Woodville was described by the insurance underwriters in 1799 as follows: "A wooden

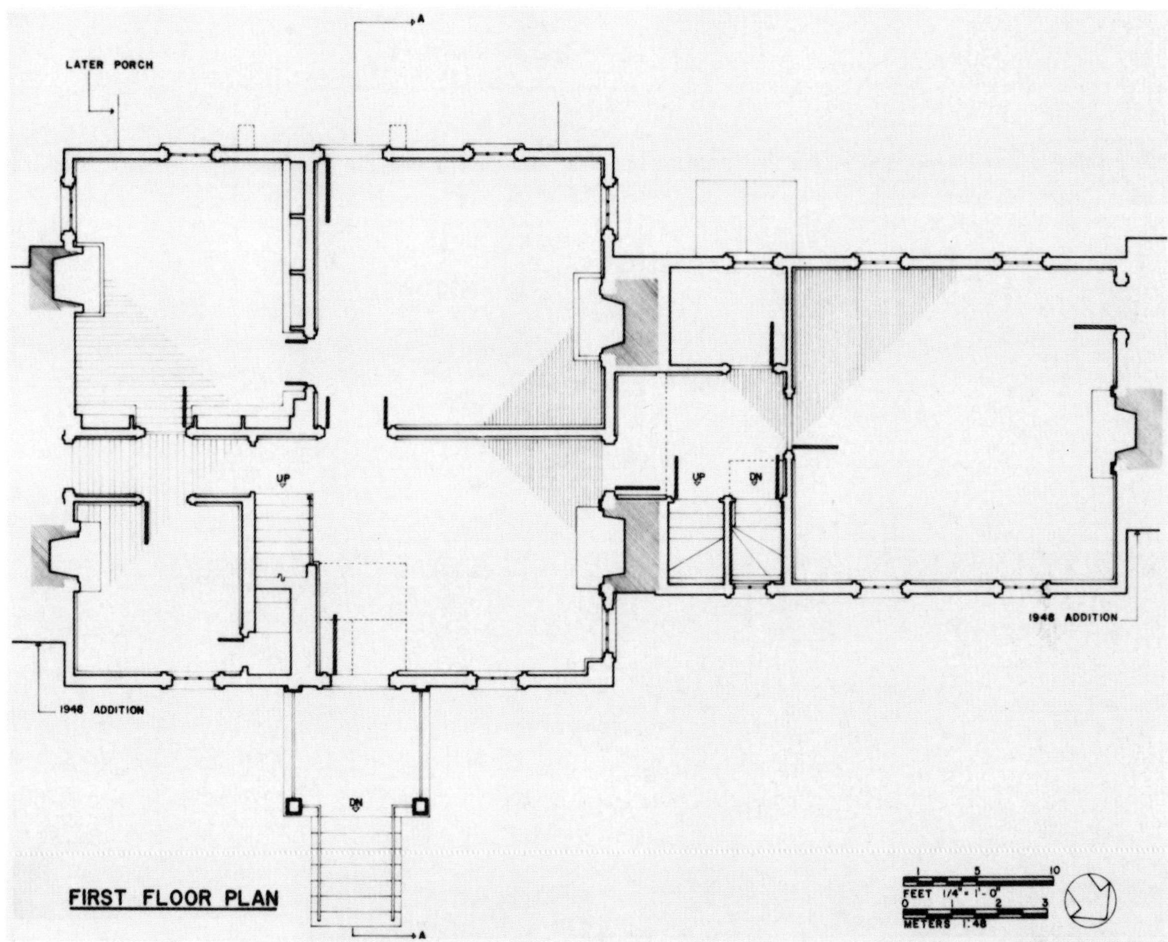

B

dwelling 36′ by 24′. Two stories high, under pinned with stone. The chimneys cover the gable ends except four feet on each side." It was valued at "Two thousand three hundred dollars in ready money, and will command the same as above specified to the best of our knowledge and belief."[9]

The plan of Woodville is interesting in the advance that it displays over the paternal house. Enniscorthy was an I house, single pile, with a chimney at each gable end. Woodville was a double-pile Georgian house with four chimneys. Only three bays long, it gives a much taller and squarer appearance than the Enniscorthy house. (See fig. 17a.) Although John's taste had advanced, it was not, one has to admit, up to the very latest thing in Federal and Jeffersonian models, as seen at Edgemont and at Monticello, houses going up at much the same period as Woodville. However, the plan and the frame construction apparently suited John Coles, and certainly it was familiar to his builder, William Bates.

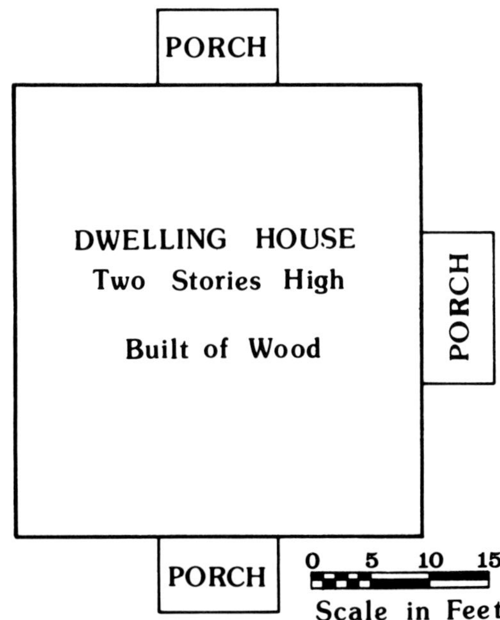

18.
Woodville: Mutual Assurance Society Records, 1810—plan of central section, valued at $3,300. (Drawn by K. Edward Lay from Mutual Assurance Society Records, no. 2275, vol. 45, reel 5, Virginia Historic Landmarks Commission, Richmond; redrawn by Patricia A. Fiedler, 1984.)

Undoubtedly, it offered an effective division of the interior living space. The first floor of the center block (fig. 17b) had four rooms, and probably a central entrance passage, which has been eliminated in the present house. Again, we must turn to the records of the Mutual Assurance Society for the original plan.[9] The drawing for 1799 shows two porches, six feet by ten feet, one on the front and the other at the back of the house. The whole structure stands on a stone cellar. Another porch, slightly larger, was added on the north side prior to 1810, as shown in the insurance voucher for that year (fig. 18). The estimated value had by then been raised to $3,300, which may reflect interior work as well as rising values.

In 1832 Walter added a single-story three-bay north wing, which is used as a dining room by the present owners. At the time of this addition, the side porch, of course, was removed, and an arch between the chimneys joins the wing with the main block of Old Woodville, so called because a second house with the same name was built nearby at a later date. Because this portion of the house remains virtually in its original form, the fine interior woodwork may still be seen. An Adamesque mantel with a wide shelf, pilasters, and full entablature dominates the dining room (fig. 19a). Federal mantels (fig. 19b), chair rails, and cornices with carved dentils adorn the rooms in the central block.

This was the house in which Walter Coles (fig. 20) lived and raised his large family.

19.
Woodville: (a) *dining-room mantel, 1832;* (b) *entrance hall, Federal mantel, c. 1796. (Photos by K. Edward Lay.)*

A

B

20.
Walter Coles, 1772–1854, oil on canvas by John Toole, 1852. (Photo by Edwin S. Roseberry from a private collection.)

ENNISCORTHY II

The adventure of Woodville, with its forward look and fine detail, can only have whetted John Coles's appetite for building. He now had ten children living, and although Walter was moving out and John III and Mary Elizabeth were soon to go, it was not at all too soon to raise the first of the many wings later to be added to Enniscorthy. The Mutual Assurance Society plan of 1799 shows a wood frame wing one story high, thirty-four feet by sixteen feet, west of the main house and joined to it by a framed covered way. (See fig. 10a.) An 1802 plan shows this wing enlarged to forty-five feet by eighteen feet, and joined directly to the central block. Another forty-six foot by eighteen foot wing has been added on the opposite end. John must have been one of Mr. Jefferson's best customers, for the account book at this time shows purchases of nails from Monticello. He also started what was to be a Coles custom, employing one of Jefferson's workmen. Hugh Chisholm did plastering both for John and for Walter.

The following account is recorded in John Coles's account book of the first phase of building Enniscorthy II.

FRANCIS WETHERED. By the amount of my Bond payable when my house was raised and covered in which became due December Albemarle Court Day 1784— 50.4	£50.4
And in 1785 Nov. John Harris	
By running up my 2 chimneys as per agreement	£11
By burning bricks	3.10
By underpinning my back porch	1
By 127 yards of seal at 5d per yd.	2.12.1
By 235 side walls @ yd	3.18.4
By your trouble in laying and cutting stones for my hearth	12
TOTAL	22.13.3

[Again in 1785] John Hall and John Harris did work, painting, bricklaying on house.

May 1786—John Harris:	
By yr. account for the work done this spring	£7.3.10
Francis Wethered	
Feb. 23, 1786: by my second bond for the piazza and extra work done on my house.	£28

July 23, 1786:	By my last bond payable when my house is finished agreeable to our bargain entered into as per bond—	£50
Henry Martin—Feb. 1785:		
	4 boxes of glass and hinges	£15.11.11
	Locks, hinges, etc.	£6.3
	By import on glass, stockings [?] and putty, locks, etc.	1.10.9
	2 mattresses	8.4.6
	Import on mattresses	7.24
	3 pieces of Irish linen	9.15.10
	By my chariott harness	72.6.6
	etc. imports and charges	13.7.7

John and Rebecca are ready to move in! Luxury items are at last making an appearance in the account book. In 1793 a "phaton" (*sic*) joined the family "chariott."[10] Wine is mentioned, only for the second time, two years later. Unlike at neighboring Monticello, wine does not seem to have been a common indulgence at Enniscorthy.

Nonetheless, there was no lack of entertainment. Sarah Coles, from Mildendo in Halifax County, wrote to her cousin Polly in Albemarle recalling "risqué riddles," and "a merry party" at Enniscorthy.[11] This was the season of spring visiting, and no doubt the Halifax young people added to the gaiety of life. It was in the same year that Isaac went off to the College of William and Mary. That John was still paying bounties on wolves at this date does not seem to have dampened social life. On these still remote plantations the occasions for socializing were limited, but all the more intensely enjoyed.

REDLANDS

Indeed, prosperity shone upon this family, as John Coles's efforts were paying off. In 1796 he bought an additional 406 acres from his neighbor William Champe Carter, and in 1797 we see him shipping 16,233 pounds of tobacco in May, and another 4,744 in October. Satisfying as all this must have been, the high point came with the marriage of John's favorite, Mary Eliza (Polly), in 1798 to Robert Carter. Robert's father, Edward Carter of Blenheim, had owned 10,000 acres in Albemarle and an Amherst County tract of about the same size. John Coles's holdings were next in size to Carter's, but even so, he was quite a way behind. After his father's death in 1792, Robert had inherited a mere 3,500 acres, but the glamor of the Carter name and his own cosmopolitan education in England made him eligible indeed. We cannot doubt that Enniscorthy did itself proud on that day, presumably lovely in early

21.
Redlands, built 1798–1810, south front. (Early twentieth-century photo, courtesy Mr. and Mrs. Robert Carter.)

May. We do know that Rebecca had a new dress. John recorded "Miss Peggy Jouett made a gown for Becky—£3-6."[12]

There was no house to speak of on Robert's land. A site had been cleared on the west side of Carter's Mountain overlooking the Hardware River, and in 1791 a small frame house had been built there. It was to this modest home, at first referred to as West Oak, that Robert and his bride now repaired.[13] Money, in this Carter generation, seems to have been short, if we can believe the complaints of Edward's widow. Our John of Enniscorthy rose to the occasion. His favorite daughter, now a Carter, should have the best house available. On August 1, 1798, a thousand pounds "was given my daughter Polly,"[14] about half of which appears to have been laid out in the first year to the account of the builder, Martin Thacker. Redlands (fig. 21) whatever the cost (and the accounts are difficult to analyze with any degree of accuracy), opens a new chapter in our study of Coles houses. Either Robert Carter or Martin Thacker, or perhaps both, was responsible for the new ideas. John himself, as the account book shows, was actively involved in paying the bills.

Curves were the wonderful new discovery; no longer was the architect confined to the straight line. Jefferson had already been to

22.
Redlands, measured drawings: (a) *south elevation;* (b) *first-floor plan;* (c) *second-floor plan;* (d) *section showing attic beams (p. 58). (Drawn by John J. Bernard, Jr., 1982, under the direction of K. Edward Lay.)*

Paris and had fallen in love, as he told Madame de Tessé, with the Hotel de Salm. At Redlands the oval drawing room and the curved entrance hall show the influence of this form on the interior plan. The handsome two-story, five-bay facade is still traditionally Georgian (fig. 22a). It is only by stepping through the door that one discovers the new inspiration. (See figs. 22b, 22c.) There is indeed something naive and altogether charming about the plan of the entrance passage. Martin Thacker's father, Nathaniel, had been a ship's carpenter. Great ceiling trusses in the attic (fig. 22d) are as heavy as any used in a ship's hull. The rounded walls of the passages from the entrance to the dining room and the master bedroom show the newer Federal influence. This entrance passage is a masterstroke, giving an airy, open feeling while retaining some privacy for the rooms beyond.

Jefferson, we know, was at home at Monticello in the midst of his

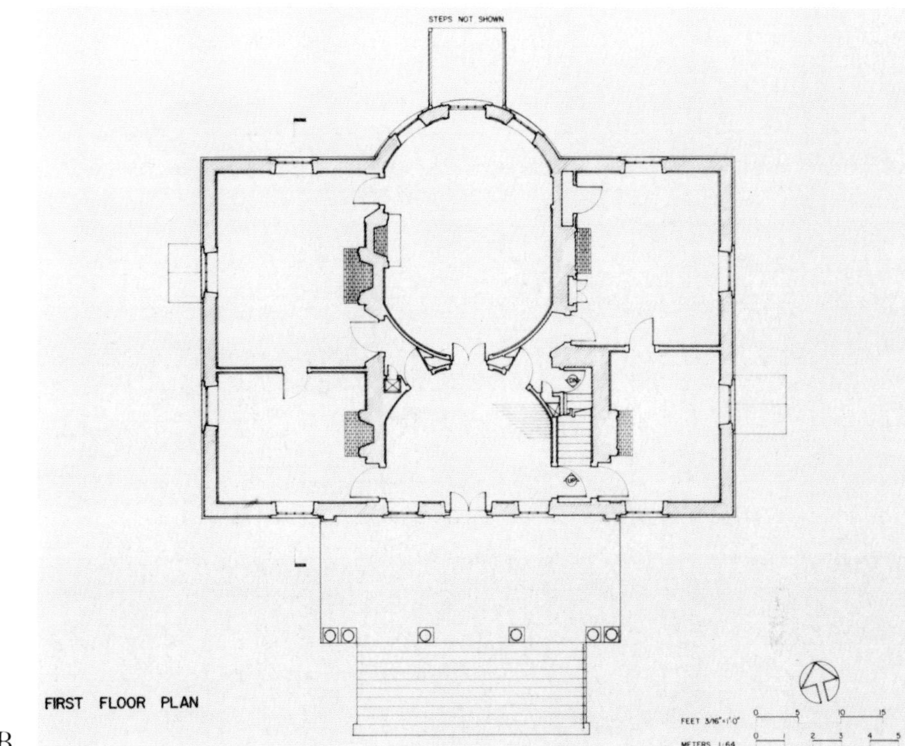
STEPS NOT SHOWN
FIRST FLOOR PLAN
FEET 3/16"=1'0"
0 5 10 15
METERS 1:64
0 1 2 3 4 5

B

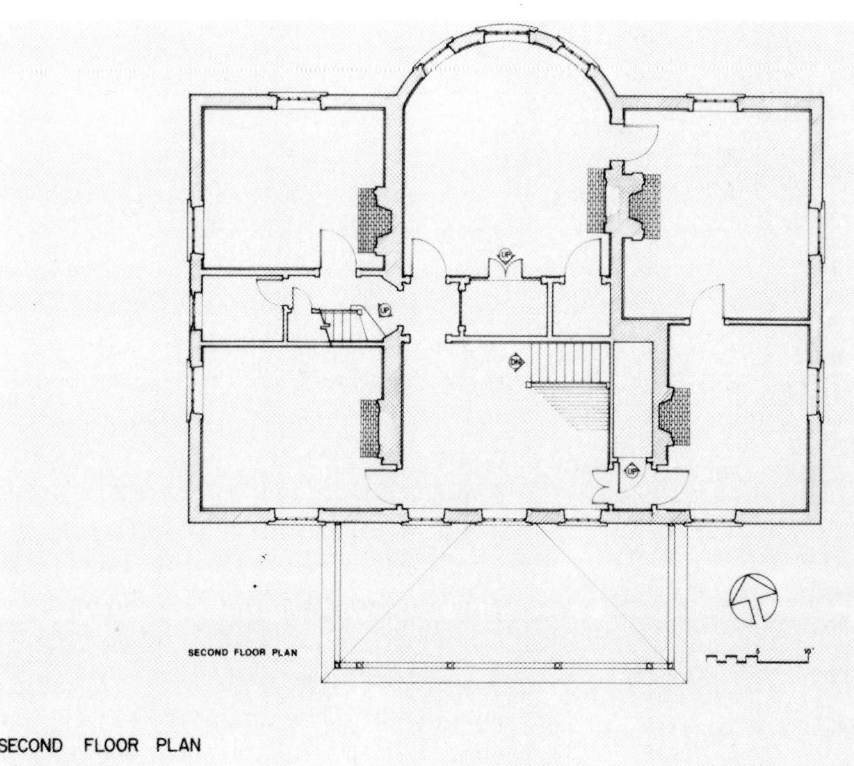
SECOND FLOOR PLAN
SECOND FLOOR PLAN
5 10'

C

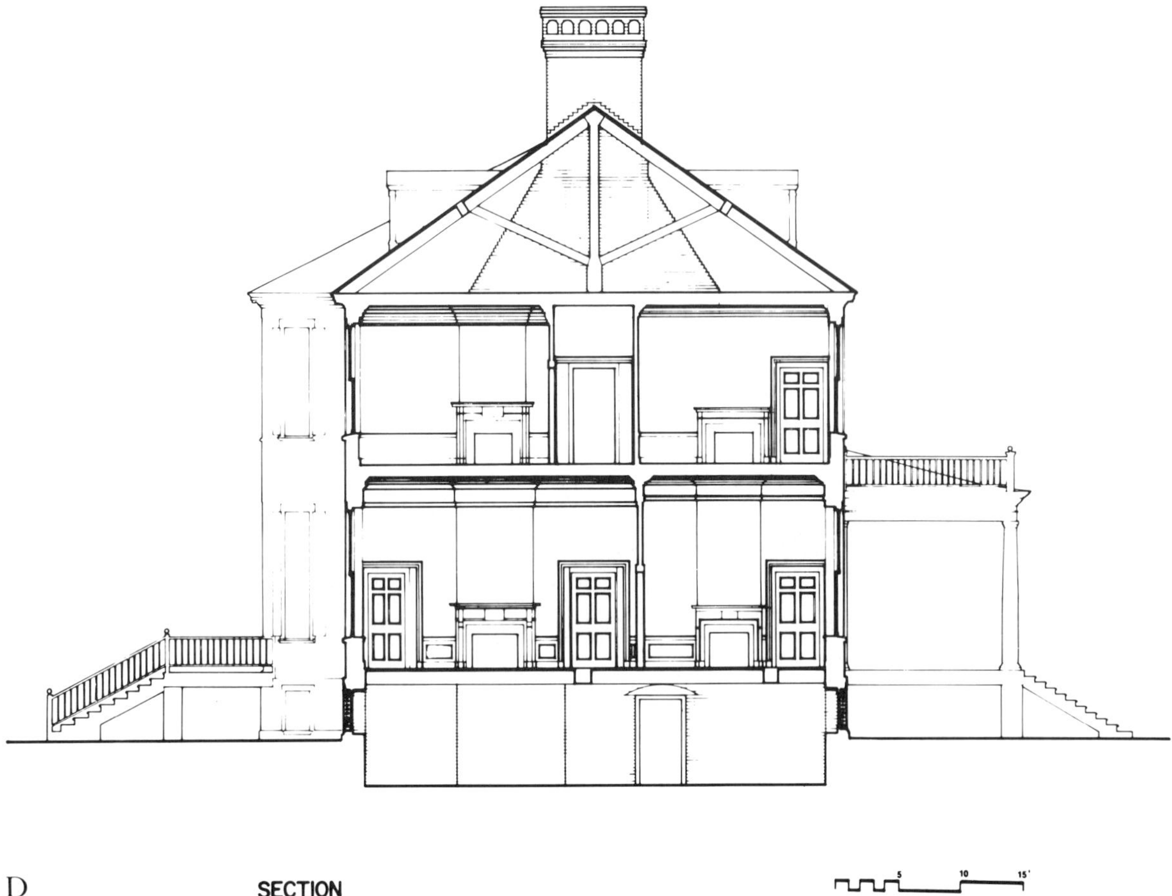

D SECTION

own remodeling when young Robert Carter returned from England. There is no surviving exchange of letters on the subject, but Robert knew the semioctagonal drawing room at Monticello, he knew those recessed and concealed stairs, and the alcove beds—all ideas that are repeated at Redlands. There is no doubt that Jefferson's spirit, with a slight Coles and Carter twist, informed this house built for the young couple at the time of their marriage in 1798. At this date the plan of the house was fixed and the work begun; it was not, however, to be completed for a number of years.

There were the usual impediments, even a law suit between Mary Eliza and the builder, Martin Thacker. John Coles had died in 1808. After Robert's death in 1809, his widow, unsure of herself and ever careful of expense, had delayed progress on the house. Martin Thacker went to work elsewhere, and Mary Eliza hired other workmen from Lynchburg, where they were then available. Thacker came back, but it is not very clear how much he was actually present. He had been

23.
Redlands, north elevation. The middle portion at the back of the house is bowed. This wall opens onto a circular porch in this 1915 photo, before the Colonial Revival changes of the 1920s. (Photo courtesy Mr. and Mrs. Robert Carter.)

promised 200 acres of Carter land as part payment for his work on Redlands, but Mary Eliza claimed that he had not fulfilled his part of the contract. Thacker won his suit in chancery.

The second-story interior was unfortunately never finished until this century, when a later version of the splendid interior woodwork was installed by Howard Sill, an associate of the well-known Colonial Revival architect John Russell Pope. Dormer windows now interrupt the original lines of the hipped roof, and the present porch has been widened across the five-bay front. The middle bays at the back of the house are bowed, following the oval curve of the drawing room within. Before the Colonial Revival changes of the twenties this wall opened onto a circular porch, three bays wide (fig. 23), which is now reduced to a single bay in width.

Some of the large forest trees remain on the lawn. The site, overlooking the southern slope and mountains to the west, had been cleared by Edward Carter's slaves in the Revolutionary period.[15] Like the Coles houses, Redlands is placed on a mountain top, with a really

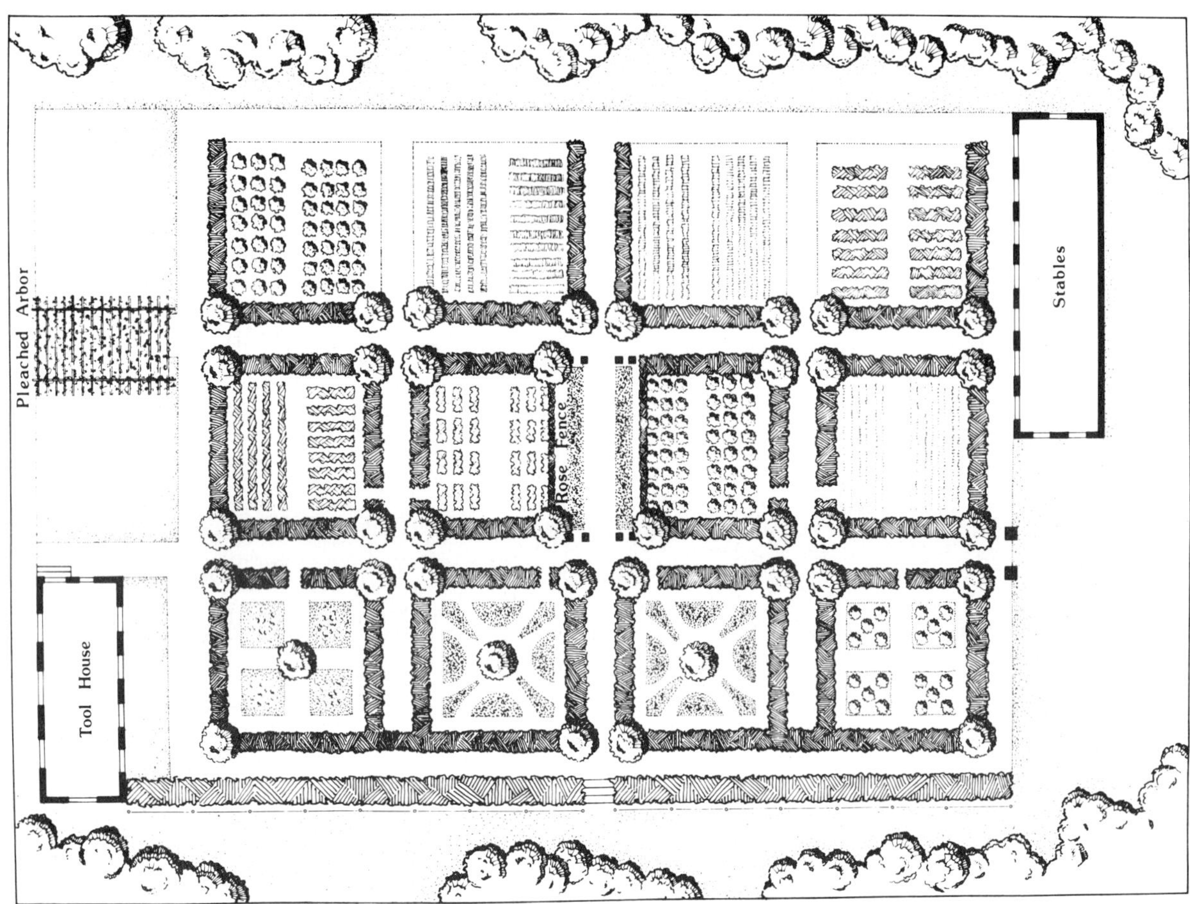

24.
Redlands: this garden located east of the house contains rectilinear beds bordered with box. A Maltese cross (Masonic symbol) appears on both sides of the central axis; the cross is planted in violets. (Drawn by Patricia A. Fiedler, 1984, based on Lila L. William's plan in James River Garden Club, Historic Gardens of Richmond *[Richmond: William Byrd Press, 1923].)*

steep drop (as at Enniscorthy) behind the house. The exterior is brick laid in penciled Flemish bond and baked from the red clay of its own mountain. The house seems to belong just where it stands, an extraordinary mixture of lightness and dignity among its old trees.

As we know, it did not go up quickly. Mary Eliza had time to plant her box bushes at the entrance to her garden and to lay it out in squares to the east of the house (fig. 24), a custom already well established at Enniscorthy. At Redlands her first two flower beds are planted in the shape of a Maltese cross, which suggests that Robert Carter may have belonged to the Masonic Order.

The interior woodwork of the first floor was done with exquisite care. In the study (fig. 25), a small room to the southwest, the mantel resembles that of brother Tucker Coles's drawing room at Tallwood (see fig. 33), who was also building at this time (around 1810). It has a rope molding and lidded urn in the center panel; the end-block consoles are in the form of a tobacco leaf, in honor of this staple crop.

25.
Redlands: southwest study, showing Federal mantel with lidded urn and tobacco-leaf end-block console. The handsome cornice displays ornate swags surrounding paterae. (Photo by Frances Benjamin Johnson, 1930s, Library of Congress.)

26.
Redlands: drawing room, showing bowed wall, Federal mantel, and cornice. (Photo by Frances Benjamin Johnson, 1930s, Library of Congress.)

Marble surrounds the brick hearth. A thirty-one inch wainscoting with raised panels runs around this room to the height of the window sills. Plaster oval paterae (sunbursts) and swags ornament the cornice frieze, all this carried off by the height of the ceiling. In a room intimate in size, this work is elaborate and elegant to an extraordinary degree.

The drawing room (fig. 26) is bowed at both ends. It is large and airy, with walk-through large sash windows on the north side. As at Monticello, they open directly to the outdoors. The fireplace here is even more impressive, five feet to the shelf of an Adamesque mantel, with decorative plaster swags matching the ceiling frieze. The Sully copy of the Stuart portrait of Wilson Cary Nicholas hangs in the place of honor over the mantel. Robert (fig. 27) and Mary Eliza (fig. 28) now hang in the dining room. The lady of this pair was not painted until 1852, when the Albemarle artist John Toole did a forceful portrait in which she appears much younger than her seventy-six years. It seems

27.
Robert Carter, 1778–1809. Oil on canvas by John Toole (possibly a posthumous portrait). (Photo by Edwin S. Roseberry.)

28.
Mary Eliza Coles Carter (Mrs. Robert Carter), 1776–1856. Oil on canvas by John Toole, 1852. (Photo by Edwin S. Roseberry.)

probable, although the second portrait is not signed, that Mary Eliza also had Toole do a posthumous version of her husband as he had looked at the time of his early death. Both look like the work of this local artist, but Mary Eliza's has the spark of life that Robert's portrait lacks. Surely the lady herself was lively. Her blunt, determined expression reflects the character of this very able woman. Robert, dying at the age of thirty-one, left little behind him, unless, indeed, it was his taste that created the fine house on Carter's Mountain.

CALYCANTHUS HILL

In the year following Polly's marriage, John II built a house for John III on the northeast end of Green Mountain, on that extension of the Green Mountain Road called Coles Rolling Road. A trace of this road, unused for a hundred and fifty years, still may be made out by the careful observer. John III attained his majority in 1795, but is not listed separately from his father on the Albemarle tax rolls until 1798, at which time he owned five adult slaves and four horses. In 1799 his house was built, frame on a stone foundation. He called it Calycanthus Hill because of the sweet shrub that grew wild all over the mountain—a shrub that was later domesticated and planted along the drive leading to the house. Its delicate fragrance greeted visitors coming up the drive, another step in the use of art in relation to landscape. There is not, however, much one can say about a house that burned to the ground in 1856 one morning while the family was in church, other than that it must have been of frame construction. The stone foundation remains, showing that his house too followed the Coles pattern, facing south, with a garden laid out to the east and cropland west of the house. No picture or description remains. It was later to be quite eclipsed by the mansion that John III built for himself and his Skipwith bride.

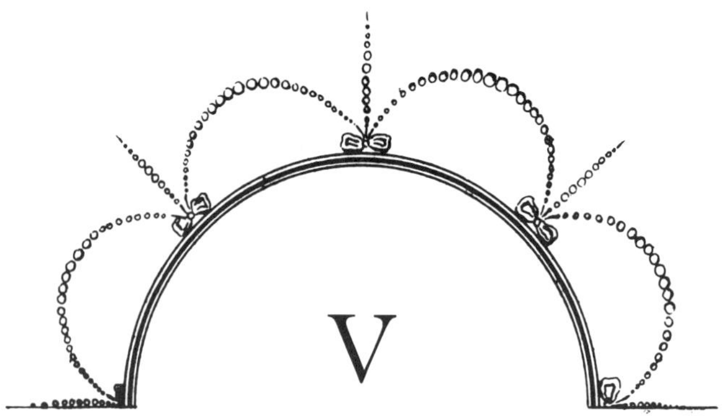

V

Enter the Skipwiths

Helen Skipwith first appears in a letter from Isaac to his friend Joseph C. Cabell. Cabell, newly married, had been extolling the joys of matrimony and had, apparently, recommended Helen to his bachelor friend. Isaac replied: "Are you really so delighted with matrimony that you would be disposed to marry your friend whether he is willing or not, and to a lady he has never seen? [This is not quite fair, as Isaac had mentioned 'H.S.' in an earlier letter to Cabell.] How very gravely you talk of this matter? Not only of the Lady, but of her 'august' mother—but it will not do—I would sooner serve a whole campaign in Mexico, then face that same august personage of whom you speak."[1]

Obviously, Lady Skipwith's reputation had preceded her. This formidable lady, nee Jean Miller, was the widow of Sir Peyton Skipwith, Bart., the only native Virginian to bear that title. Sir Peyton and his lady had built a handsome house, Prestwould, on the Roanoke River in Mecklenburg County, which in a sense we may think of as the Coles's motherhouse, for two Skipwith girls were to marry Coles men. Evidently brother Tucker did not share Isaac's sentiments, for it was he who went courting to Mecklenburg. He had not at first been smiled upon by the august lady of the house. Lady Skipwith wrote a friend asking, in effect, if Tucker was after Helen for her money. When reassured on this point, she gave her consent. The marriage took place in 1810, when the Coles were entertained at a state dinner at Prestwould. Rebecca has left a rather appalled description of the occasion:

We did not enter the dining room until candle light when, instead of meat and vegetables, the table was covered with artificial flowers, pictures, oranges, sugar candy, nuts, wine, and silver vases of hot water to set plates on. We all took our seats and found a piece of bread wrapped up in a nice napkin, and a gold spoon and silver knife and fork by the side of all our plates.

29.
Tallwood, 1804–34, home of Tucker and Helen Skipwith Coles. (Photo by Frances Benjamin Johnson, 1930s, Library of Congress.)

Presently they brought from the next room soup in plates for everybody; then the plates were changed and we all had a piece of turkey and one vegetable and so continued until the plates were changed fifteen times for the meat course and twelve times for the desert.[2]

Such were the hazards of a Skipwith alliance.

It would sometimes seem that this lady would have liked to unbend, but did not know how. Her library, chosen entirely by herself, was one of the finest of the period in Virginia—certainly by far the finest collected by a woman. The extent of her garden (recently restored) and her garden journals have long excited the admiration of experts. But there it was. She remained "august," and no one, not even her children, ever thought of her as lovable.

Helen Skipwith, arriving at Enniscorthy, can hardly believe her reception. "Such another family scarcely exists.... Our mother [Rebecca] is a charming old lady of upwards of fifty.... She is almost worshipped by us all . . . her manners are so soft and affable that you are made *friend* ere you become her acquaintance."[3]

TALLWOOD

Tucker at the time of his marriage had been able to bring his bride to a home of their own. Tallwood (fig. 29) was the third dwelling house that John Coles built for his children on his land on the Green Mountain. The house is on the Green Mountain Road between Enniscorthy and Old Woodville. As do all the Coles houses, it faces south on a ridge that slopes gradually to the north—although not as steeply here as on the Enniscorthy and Redlands sites. In 1804 and 1805 John II was putting in large orders for building materials. Some material may have been for his own additions at Enniscorthy, but as an order to Thurston I. Dickerson for exactly the number of bricks needed to build the two chimneys for the central block at Tallwood is dated November 1805, it seems pretty clear that the original house was finished at about this date. Interior evidence shows that the core of what was later to become the mansion at Tallwood (see fig. 30) was at first only a single-pile, story-and-a-half structure, sheathed with beaded weatherboards covering brick nogging, a form of insulation used at the period. This was the house that Helen referred to when, as a bride, she was asked the name of her new home. "It's such a little house," she said, "it has no name."

The second Coles-Skipwith marriage did not occur until some twelve years later, when John III, then a bachelor of forty-eight, married Helen's younger sister, Selina. Selina, aged twenty-nine at the time of her marriage, had been in love with her cousin, a young naval officer, but Lady Skipwith had told her firmly, "If a man wishes to keep a canary, he must have a cage to put her in." Selina's lover had only his ship. She married John Coles, and made the best of it.

When Jean Skipwith died in 1826, the fortunes of the John and Tucker Coles families enjoyed a dramatic change. To her daughters Lady Skipwith left $30,000 each, in "good bonds," in addition to some well-trained slaves (mason Dick, Richard, a carpenter, and so forth), and two hundred volumes each from her magnificent library. To Tucker Coles, the only person not of her own blood mentioned in her will, she left "my domestic medicine chest (by Maxwell) also the Encyclopedia Britannica in Twenty Vol. Quarto."[4] She recognized a community of interests in the master of Tallwood.

Lady Skipwith had indeed proved herself a woman of business acumen. Her estate amounted to something between four and five

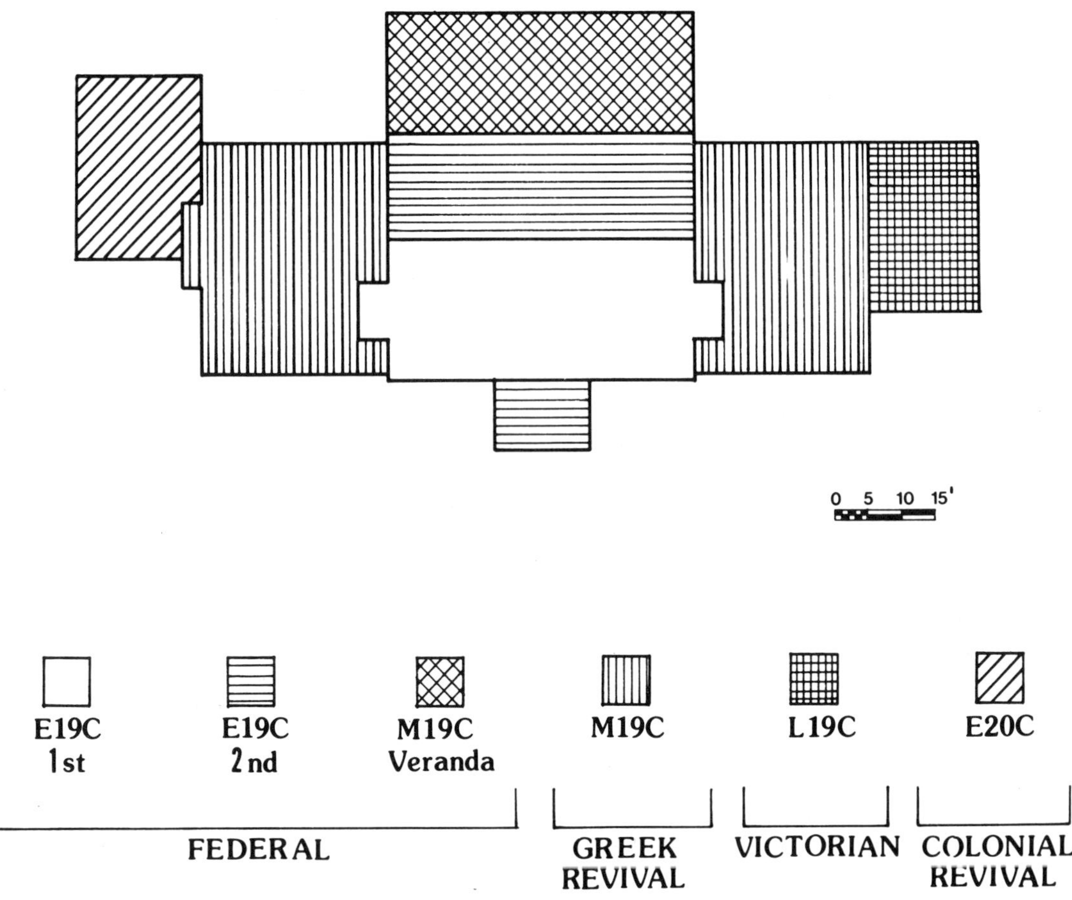

30.
Plan showing chronology of Tallwood buildings. (drawn by K. Edward Lay, 1983; redrawn by Patricia A. Fiedler, 1984.)

hundred thousand dollars; the bonds left to her daughters were her own, not acquired from the estate of her husband. Hugh Miller, Jean's merchant father, had returned with most of his fortune to Scotland; as her share of his estate she had inherited £1,000 sterling. During her widowhood she had bought land, but she had also bought additional bonds, so that after her death the Coles interests were not limited to land and slaves, and so perhaps they escaped some of the problems connected with a declining plantation economy.

We may conclude that such a decline was endemic to a population heavily weighted with slaves and "poor whites." The concentration of wealth in the hands of the planters failed to provide an important home market; lacking sufficient imports, Virginia's export trade and much of its profit—on which, of course, she relied—were being siphoned off, going through New York and the New England ports.[5] The planters were selling cheap, while new protective tariffs were forcing them to buy at high prices. Internal improvements in the form of increased facilities for transportation to the western markets might have alleviated the situation, but the slave owners, although agreeing that change was necessary, could not accept the form of taxation necessary to put the change into effect. Isaac, Mary Eliza Carter, Tucker, and John were no exception to the rule. This generation of Coles made no effort to improve on the plantation system. They traveled, they knew more of the world than their parents, but still first among pleasures were the mighty family reunions at Enniscorthy.

In 1829, for example, Miss Betsy Coles's diary[6] shows them all reunited: married sisters Rebecca Coles Singleton from South Carolina, Sally Coles Stevenson and Emily Ann Coles Rutherfoord from Richmond with their husbands and children, all under brother Isaac's hospitable roof. Old Rebecca had died in that watershed year of 1826, so that Isaac and his unmarried sister Betsy were now Enniscorthy's hosts. The builders of the fine plantation houses have often been accused of conspicuous consumption, but as plantations had to be socially as well as economically self sufficient, we can hardly doubt that "the big house" played an important role. The Coles certainly had traditions of fine building on both sides of the family, which they now set out to emulate. At Tallwood it was a matter of additions; John and Selina were to start afresh, with the handsome brick mansion that they called Estouteville, after a noble Norman ancestor of the Skipwith family.

Tallwood's second story had probably been a part of the house described by Helen at her marriage in 1810. (By 1820 the house was valued for tax purposes at $2,000.) The lovely two-storied Federal portico is an integral part of the central block, and would have been added by 1810 or shortly thereafter. The great leap in building value from $2,000 to nearly $9,000 in 1826–27 marks the major addition of the two Greek Revival wings. (See fig. 31a, b.) It is a part of the almost miraculous success of Tallwood's piecemeal building that the portico that worked so well on the original central block remains a beautiful focal point on the greatly extended facade. Perhaps Tucker and Helen had planned it so. The north or back side of the house was extended to include a long cellar passage running the length of the building and supporting a long passage and additional rooms above. The concept of the cellar corridor is also found at Estouteville, Monticello, and Bremo. With these additions Tallwood would have seemed nearly complete, one of the finest federal frame houses in Virginia, but there was yet more to come.

In the spring of 1834 Helen wrote to her sister-in-law Lelia Skipwith that "some little matter of building"[7] would prevent their visit to

A

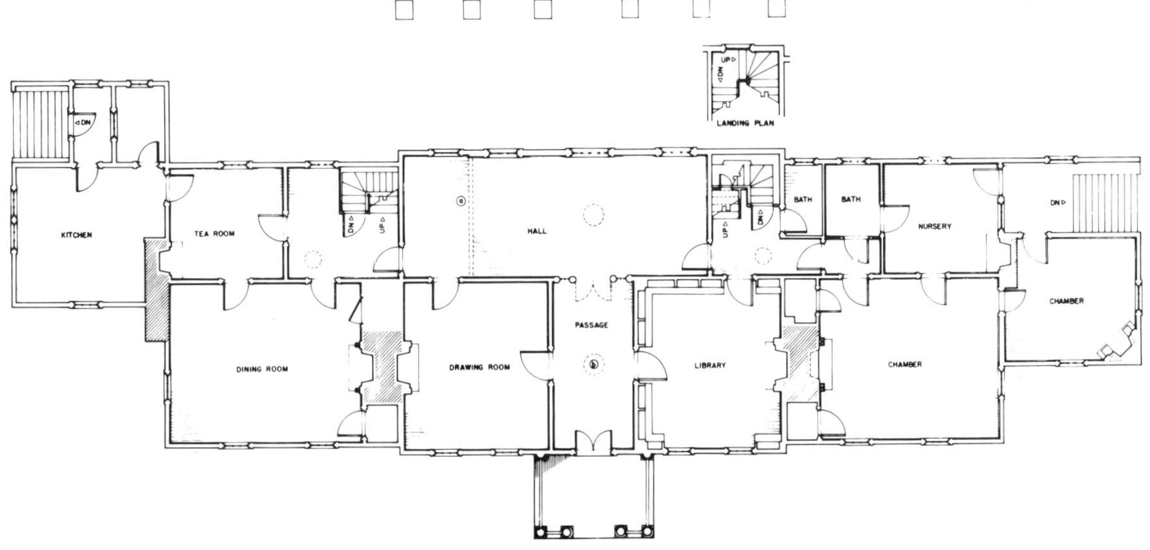

B

31.
Tallwood, measured drawings: (a) *south elevation;* (b) *first floor. (Drawn by Lisa Umstattd, under the direction of K. Edward Lay, 1981.)*

32.
Tallwood piazza, c. 1900. (Photo courtesy Darrah Alger.)

Prestwould that summer. While shopping for furniture in Philadelphia in the following spring, Helen wrote to Selina asking "What Bowles is engaged about—whether he has received the box of hardware—Whether the porch is in progress, etc.?—"[8] We can assume that "the porch" refers to that finishing touch, a piazza (fig. 32) running the length of the central block, recalling the piazza at Enniscorthy. A row of Tuscan columns and a railing adorned the one at Tallwood. When the fields were all cleared and cultivated, as they were when Tucker and Helen sat there, it is said that one could see the Rotunda in Charlottesville on a clear day. Nothing now remains of the view or the viewing place.

The interior photographs of Tallwood show the simple but lovely Federal mantel in the drawing room, completed c. 1810 (fig. 33). The lidded urn in the center panel and the end-block consoles in the form of a tobacco leaf recall the same treatment at Redlands. (See fig. 25.) In figure 34 we see a mantel of a later period in the Greek Revival dining room. Here too was the punkah, the great fan hung over the dining-room table and operated by a Negro boy pulling a rope, standing out of

33.
Tallwood: drawing room, showing a Federal mantel similar to one in the study at Redlands (see fig. 25). (Photo by Frances Benjamin Johnson, 1930s, Library of Congress.)

34.
Tallwood: dining room showing the punkah brought from India by Fulwar Skipwith, Helen Coles's nephew. (Photo by Frances Benjamin Johnson, 1930s, Library of Congress.)

35.
John Coles III, 1774–1848, of Estouteville: chalk on paper, 1808, by Saint-Mémin. (Photo by Edwin S. Roseberry.)

sight in the back hall. The gentle breeze thus produced cooled the guests and kept flies from the table. Fulwar Skipwith, traveling in India in 1857, had sent this useful gift to his sister Helen. It offered what we may consider the ultimate in personal service.

ESTOUTEVILLE

While Tucker and Helen were engaged in building at Tallwood, John (fig. 35) and Selina (fig. 36) were equally busy at Estouteville. The building at Estouteville was started in 1827; it was completed in 1830. Here they were building an entirely new house, uninhibited by any

36.
Selina Skipwith Coles (Mrs. John Coles III), 1793–1870, of Estouteville: oil on wood panel, by L. M. D. Guillaume, 1857. (Photo by Edwin S. Roseberry.)

attempt to remodel a previous structure. They hired Jefferson's principal builder, James Dinsmore, who had recently been engaged in remodeling Montpelier (fig. 37) for the Madisons. John and Selina must have been pleased with Dinsmore's work at Montpelier, for their own interior plan followed it in many respects, including the long passage connecting the wings at the rear of the house. The brickwork was done by William B. Phillips, a leading brickmason employed by Jefferson to work with Dinsmore at the University of Virginia.[9] As with all previous Coles houses, Estouteville was placed on a high ridge, facing south, although in this case the front turns slightly to the

37.
Montpelier, home of James Madison, remodeled by James Dinsmore, c. 1810. (Photo, Library of Congress.)

western mountains. The site is close to and just a bit higher than the old house at Calycanthus Hill. The Green Mountain road runs through the property on the west side of the house, dividing the lawn from barns and cropland below the road. Tall tulip poplars older than the house shade this lawn. One can see as far as the James River to the south; like John II before him it was to Scott's Ferry (now called Scottsville) that John III carried his tobacco.

The main approach is from what was then called the Staunton–James River Turnpike. Our first sight of the house as we approach up a long drive will be the commanding Roman Revival portico, four columns wide (figs. 38, 39a, b, c). There is an identical portico at the back on the north side. The two-story central block, raised above half windows on the cellar level, is seven bays wide; two one-storied wings of three bays each balance the facade. A hip roof completes the simple yet strongly integrated design. Jefferson, of course, never saw his friend's house, yet his influence is as clearly seen here as at Redlands,

38.
Estouteville, south elevation: architect-builder James Dinsmore, 1828–30. (Photo by Frances Benjamin Johnson, 1930s, Library of Congress.)

although with quite different results. Like John Hartwell Cocke's Bremo, Estouteville was built by one of Jefferson's builders; the Coles employed James Dinsmore, while John Nielson was the architect-builder at Bremo. Perhaps Estouteville is more *American*, less subtle, than some of Jefferson's own work, but in its own setting—the portico approached directly through its great trees—it is unsurpassed.

The interior woodwork has been most carefully executed. The great hall (fig. 40), particularly fine, was referred to as the "summer living room." Like Tuckahoe and Stratford Hall, it has no fireplace. Running the width of the house and opened at both ends by double three-paneled doors, it catches every summer breeze. The doors are surmounted by segmental fanlights similar to those used by brother Tucker at Tallwood. At Estouteville the doors are flanked by triple-

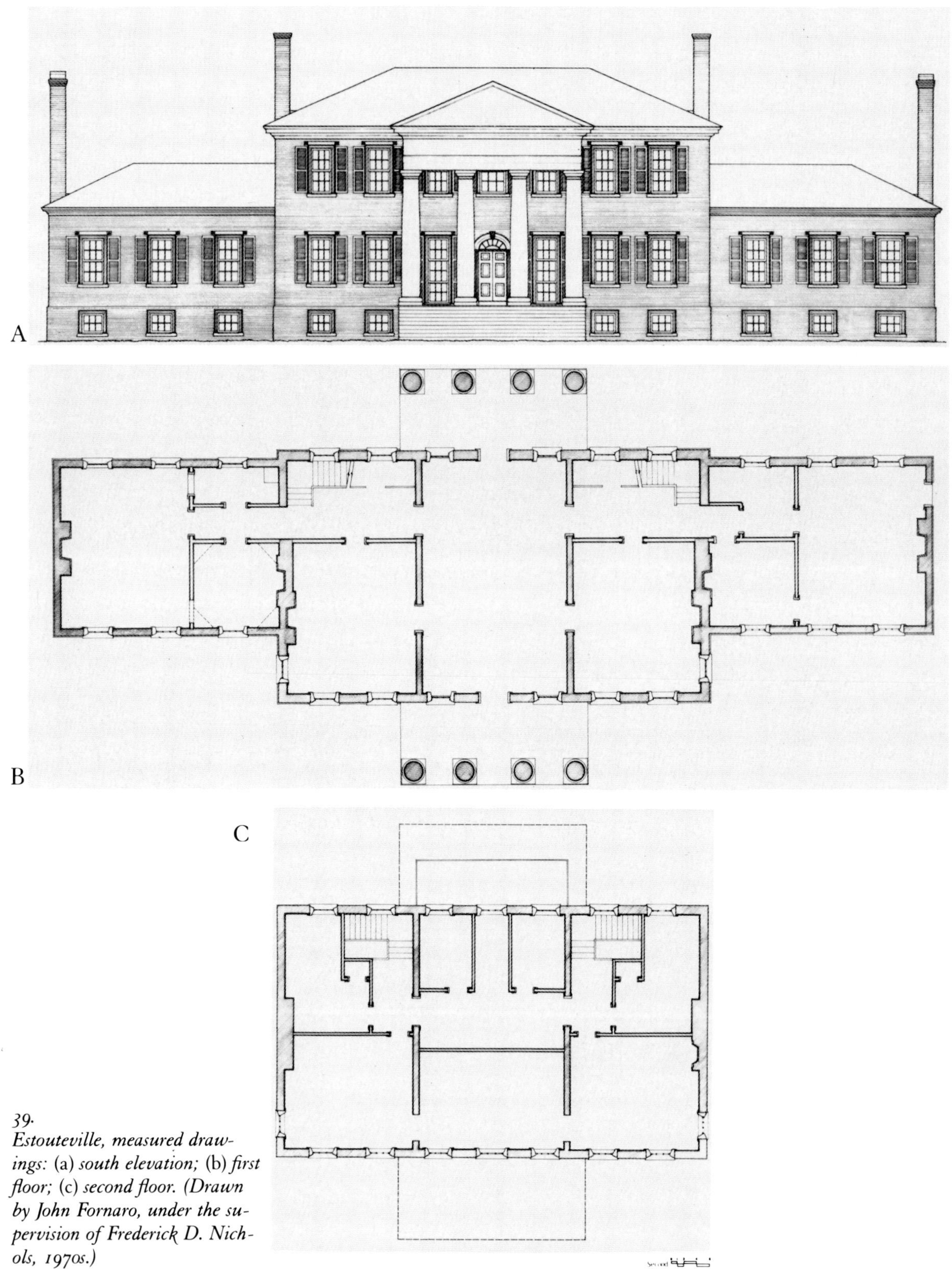

39.
Estouteville, measured drawings: (a) *south elevation;* (b) *first floor;* (c) *second floor. (Drawn by John Fornaro, under the supervision of Frederick D. Nichols, 1970s.)*

40.
Estouteville: great hall, showing cornice with ox-skull frieze. (Photo by Frances Benjamin Johnson, 1930s, Library of Congress.)

hung windows, completing the open feeling of this so rightly called summer living room.

The space thus enclosed is thirty-five feet by twenty-three feet with a thirteen-foot ceiling, firmly delineated by a deep entablature. The proportions are perfect; in the words of Calder Loth, the Estouteville hall is "the noblest room in Virginia."[10] The frieze is decorated with bucrania (ox skulls) set between triglyphs, a design taken by Jefferson from the illustrated Leoni edition of Palladio. Palladio's design (fig. 41a) was taken from the Roman Temple of Vesta, goddess of the hearth and of plenty, an appropriate design for the farm-oriented Coles. Jefferson's designs, were, of course, well known to Dinsmore.

The bucrania are traditionally supposed to have been carved in wood by Hessian craftsmen, descendants of those prisoners of war who remained in the county after the Revolution. This all too familiar tale

41.
Pattern book designs used at Estouteville: (a) *Andrea Palladio, 1508–1580,* The Architecture of A. Palladio; in four books, *translated from the Italian original, 2nd edition (London:* Vignette, *1721), bk. 1, pl. 1570. (Manuscript note on title page: "This copy of the work from which Mr. Jefferson made his drawings of the Rotunda and the Pavilions of the University of Virginia is presented to the University of Virginia with the homage of Thomas Nelson Page.")* (b) *Asher Benjamin,* The American Builders Companion *(Charlestown, Mass.: printed by S. Etheridge, Junr., 1811.), pl. 36.* (c) *Asher Benjamin,* The Practical House Carpenter, Being a Complete Development of the Grecian Orders of Architecture *(Boston: the author, 1830.) pl. 47.*

A

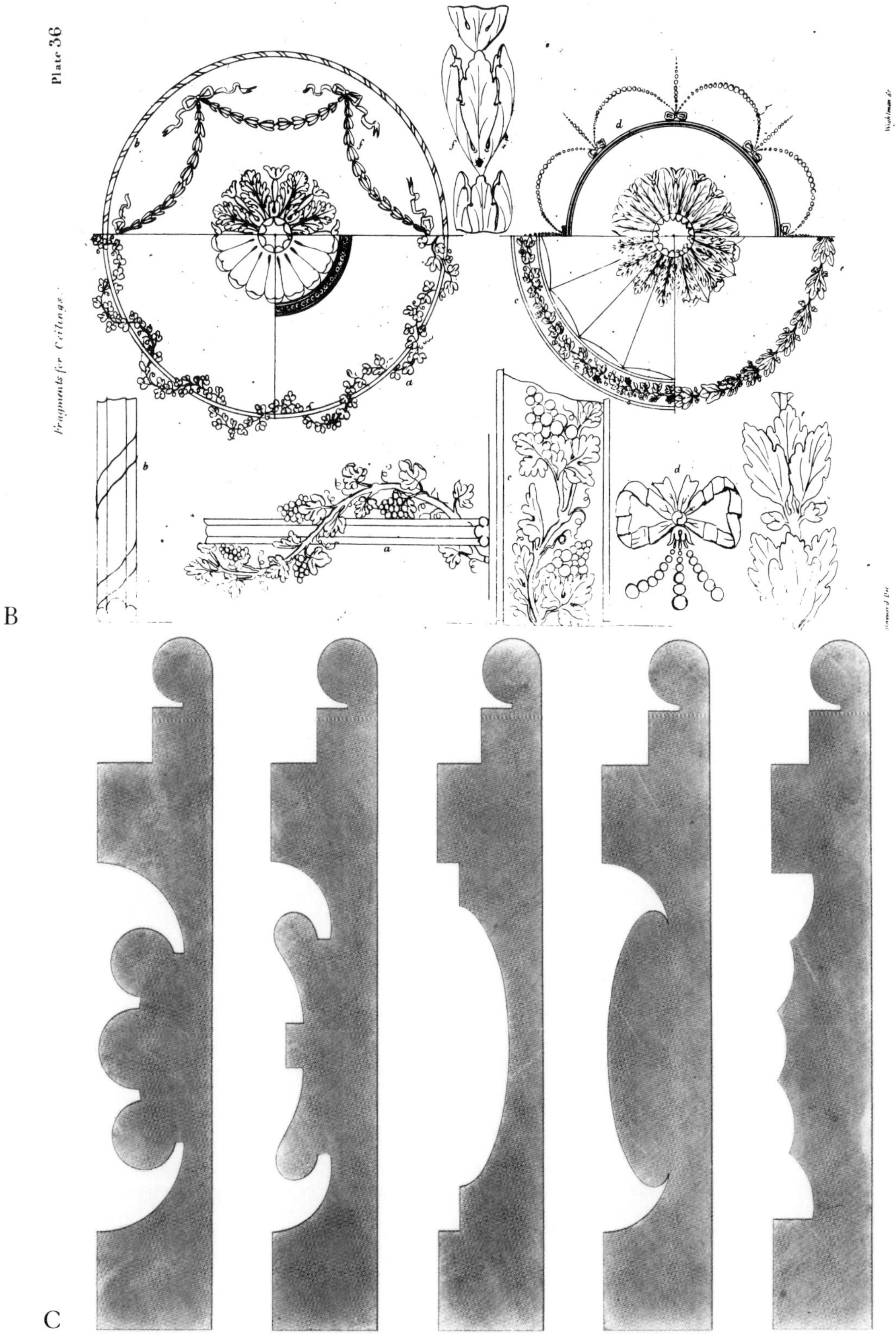

B

C

may be readily disproved at Estouteville, where the skulls are made of a composite substance resembling plaster, poured into a mold and allowed to dry. This was the method used by William J. Coffee, who besides his little portrait busts, did all the ornamental work used by Jefferson at the University of Virginia. It is tempting to attribute the bucrania at Estouteville to Coffee. John Coles had known him of old, and he was a fellow worker with Dinsmore at the university, but without documentation we cannot be sure. The plaster medallion on the ceiling is an ornament taken from the pattern book of Asher Benjamin (fig. 41b).

That the Coles themselves were well aware of these sources of inspiration may be seen in a letter from Isaac to his friend John Hartwell Cocke at Bremo:

> With Mr. Jefferson I conversed at length on the subject of architecture. Palladio he said "was the Bible." You should get it and stick close to it. He disapproved of parapet walls—no House could be made perfectly tight with them. . . . The roof should cover the walls & the Balustrade could be raised above it as at Monticello which tho not handsome was safe [an unaccustomed view of T.J. as a practical builder]. . . . [Another rule] was the height of a room should be equal to its width. . . . The Tuscan order was too plain—it would do for your barns, etc., but was not fit for a dwelling House—the Doric would not cost much more & would be vastly handsomer—his was doric. You could get drawings of the columns, cornice, etc., etc. from him. Dinsmore he recommends to you as a good and faithful workman. . . . would build you a House without any false architecture, so much the rage at present. (He is a great advocate for light and air. . . .) I cannot recollect, much less write the one half of what he said to me, but when we meet . . . I will repeat much more of our conversation.[11]

Besides showing the Roman character of much of Jefferson's architectural ideas, this letter points up a relationship that has always been most difficult to document. How much of the design specifically was the work of the builder and how much that of the owner? We see the position of the builder gradually increasing in status until we may think of Nielson and Dinsmore (although Jefferson speaks of Dinsmore as a "workman") as architect-builders. Isaac's letter represents the owners; it shows the very intensive and no doubt decisive interest in architectural matters taken by the owners themselves.

In the brief period 1827–32 all of the Coles brothers, with the exception of Edward, were building: John at Estouteville, Tucker at Tallwood, and Walter, who was adding a room at Old Woodville. John and Tucker were both on the building committee planning the new church at Glendower. The specifications for the latter building, preserved in the Coles papers, are particularly specific (see chapter seven, below). There is no way to escape the conclusion that there was considerable consultation in regard to the plan of the church between the committee and their builder, and probably suggestions came from both sides. Clearly pattern books were also consulted for the fine points of design, which were then adopted.

Naturally not every recommendation contained in Isaac's leter to Cocke was applied to Estouteville, but many were. Dinsmore, and probably John III, had no interest in a balustrade, even in one perched safely, if not handsomely, on a pitched roof. The original hip roof of imported German tin, as recommended by Jefferson,[12] covered Estouteville for more than a hundred and fifty years and has just been replaced in copper by the present owners. The handsome Doric columns of the porticoes do in fact follow the advice given to Isaac. As at Monticello, the fanlighted doorway, glimpsed through columns, gives an effect of lightness, relieving the monumental character of the columns.

Entering the house through the great hall, we find symmetrically placed rooms on either side. A passage runs the length of the house at the rear, as far as the two end rooms, so that standing in the dining room (fig. 42), one can look more than a hundred feet to the master bedroom (fig. 43) beyond. As at Monticello a pair of stairs rise unobtrusively from this passage to the second story, so that the great hall may remain an uncluttered space. The Greek Revival architrave trim surrounding doors and windows are a bit surprising in this Jeffersonian house; it is especially interesting, as it represents a very early use in Virginia of this new Grecian trend. Shortly before his untimely death by drowning in 1830, James Dinsmore must have acquired the revised edition, just out, of Asher Benjamin's book *The Practical House Carpenter, Being the Complete Development of the Grecian Orders of Architecture.*

Figure 41c shows the trim used at Estouteville in every room but the pantry, an insignificant room that may actually have been finished after Dinsmore's death. The window side moldings are splayed throughout, that is, set at an angle with paneled insets, designed to admit additional light. We remember Mr. Jefferson's fondness for light and air. The mantels in the two end rooms have wall-of-Troy moldings, producing, appropriate to the ceiling height, a more massive impression than those at Tallwood.

Besides being a builder and a successful planter, John III was a precise man of business. Although itemized accounts are not available, we have an extraordinarily detailed balance sheet of profit and loss for the years 1816 through 1838. Unlike Mr. Jefferson, John Coles knew to

42.
Estouteville: dining room, showing mantel with wall-of-Troy dentils, original pillar-and-claw table from Needles of Baltimore, and large china press. (Photo by Frances Benjamin Johnson, 1930s, Library of Congress.)

43.
Estouteville: master bedroom, first floor, showing mahogany wardrobes made for this room by Needles of Baltimore in 1830. (Photo by Frances Benjamin Johnson, 1930s, Library of Congress.)

the last penny where he stood. For only five of these twenty-three years did he spend less than his income; most of his outgo, however, was in the form of capital investment: land, building, and stocks and bonds. In 1827, for example, the plantation showed a profit of $4,572.79, about half of which came from the sale of tobacco: $2,337.63. In this year he was working thirty-seven slaves. Interest on stocks and bonds came to another quarter of his total income: $1,223.33. But this was the great year of building the new mansion house: there was $4,833.30 in building expenses. In the two following years there were additional building expenses of approximately $2,700 and $2,800 respectively. Total cost of the Estouteville house probably reached $10,000. (In 1831 property lists valued his improvements at $10,000, and total buildings at $18,000. This last figure would include Calycanthus Hill.)

In a personal way John and Selina were not extravagant. In 1827 we

44.
Federal mahogany desk, c. 1810–20, used by Helen Coles at Tallwood. (Photo by Edwin S. Roseberry from a private collection.)

see "Clothes for Self": $178.81, and "Clothes for Selina": $161.20. "Newspapers and Books" amounted to only $17. One hopes that they were busy reading the volumes recently inherited from Jean Skipwith! We could do a similar analysis for each of these twenty-three years, but perhaps it is enough to remark that both income and expenses went up regularly year by year, with the exception of building costs, which after 1830 were virtually nonexistent.

Having achieved a house as fine as any in the state, John and Selina now naturally turned their attention to furniture. The solid pieces bought by Helen and Selina fit the spaces for which they were intended. Nor were the older pieces totally eliminated. Helen's little desk (fig. 44), valued at $10 in the inventory of her estate, was known to have come from Prestwould, probably at the time of her marriage. Obviously, a good deal of fine furniture still surviving in the family dates from the eighteenth century. From around 1810–15 there is a particularly graceful set of Duncan Phyfe scroll-back side chairs with carved eagles placed head to head in the back (fig. 45a, b). In all probability these chairs came originally from Enniscorthy, although

45.
(a) *Duncan Phyfe scroll-back side chair, 1810–15;* (b) *detail of chair: splat with carved eagles. (Private collection.)*

A

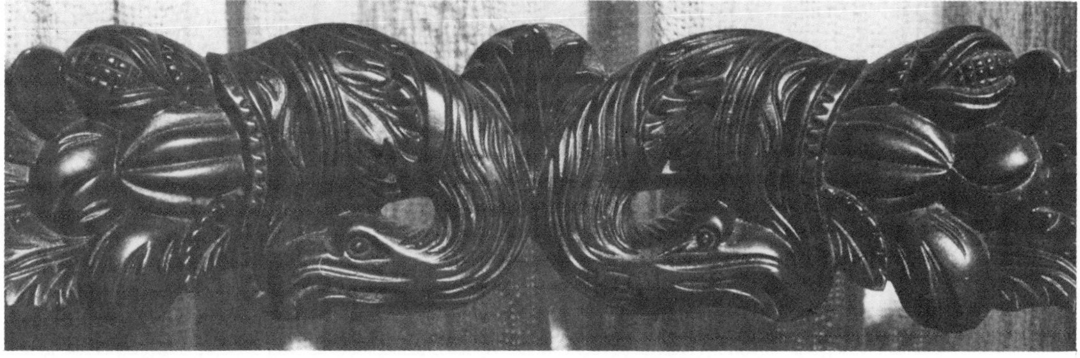

B

46.
French Empire dressing stand originally from Prestwould. (Photo by Edwin S. Roseberry from a private collection.)

they could have been bought by Tucker and Helen. A French Empire dressing stand (fig. 46), on the other hand, is known to have come from Prestwould. There is a fine Duncan Phyfe sofa (fig. 47) of the same 1810–15 date, with reeded legs and reeded arm supports. A Federal card table, decanters and champagne glasses, silver coin spoons, and a silver ladle by Armistead Truslow of Lynchburg (shown in fig. 12) were all a part of the amenities of life as lived by this generation of the family.

By the time that Selina had begun to buy furniture for Estouteville, her purchases, 1830–35, are amply documented in Helen's correspon-

47.
Duncan Phyfe sofa, 1810–15. (Photo by Edwin S. Roseberry from a private collection.)

dence with her sister. It was Helen who did the shopping, passing on her discoveries to her sister at home. Tucker's frail health (he lived to age seventy-nine) took them often to Philadelphia, where of course everyone who was anyone in the South took their complaints to the famous Dr. Physick. Helen improved these opportunities by visiting the best cabinetmakers and marblemasons in both Philadelphia and Baltimore. That Selina was considering marble mantels for the upstairs bedrooms at Estouteville is clear from a letter of 1828:

> We stopped first at Struthers when we saw some [mantels] at $250-$200-150—& two exactly alike of beautiful grey American marble for $100 each—to which we both gave a decided preference—others of inferior quality at more reduced prices—we then proceeded to Williams—his work is perhaps not so beautiful as that of the other shop but far cheaper—for instance he offered us very neat American marble mantles [*sic*] suited to your chamber with freestone hearths complete for $45—he is enabled to work at more reduced rates, from the fact of having a very powerful engine worked by steam power.[13]

Whether Selina succumbed to the blandishments of the machine age for the upstairs mantels we cannot now tell, for they have been replaced, but happily for her own chamber she used the large mantel with wall-of-Troy dentils, a match to the one in the dining room. The pair of beautiful mahogany wardrobes (see fig. 43) made by John Needles, cabinetmaker of Baltimore, was bought in 1830. Here the evidence is preserved in Needles own label still glued inside the doors.

We may be glad of these priceless labels, although their survival does contradict the family tradition that the Needles wardrobes were packed with silver and sunk beneath the James to save them from Sheridan's raiders.

In 1835 Helen was once more shopping in earnest for both Selina and herself. She was in Baltimore with Isaac and Julia in May, and their most productive stop is again at the famous shop of Needles. She ordered:

> [Two] tables [see fig. 42], pillar and claw—with an extra leaf for extraordinary occasions. They will cost $100. . . . All articles much higher as you proceed North—our purchases will be made here and sent on in the freight boats—we shall omit many articles contained in our list . . . even then the mahogany furniture will cost upwards of $1000, beyond which I am not willing to go. . . . [As to] carpets: Brussels we find is $1.75, Kidderminster $1.25, Stair 75¢ (narrow).[14]

An early photograph of the great hall shows strips of carpeting, which may indeed have been the Kidderminster referred to.

Smaller purchases made in Philadelphia were "scalloped dishes" (fig. 48a) and "two Astral Lamps for your [Selina's] Hall Tables—they give a beautiful light—are easily managed, and will impart quite a different appearance to your Hall—with nice cut [glass] shades the pair cost $21—and are exceedingly cheap . . . from Richmond we will forward a little good oil for them." In a later letter, June 20, she informed Selina that they had found two other pairs, similar but much handsomer, at $24. They were indeed handsome, and survive today (fig. 48b), without, alas, their original glass shades. They have been converted to electricity and have also lost their receptacle for oil; nevertheless, they are still handsome.

Decorating the hall presented a challenge. There was the fine plaster ceiling medallion adapted from Asher Benjamin's pattern book, and Selina had her tables and her astral lamps, but how to treat the walls beneath the bucrania frieze? Her brother Humberston had been decorating his walls at Prestwould with the beautiful French scenic paper imported by Regnault of Richmond.[15] Selina could have done the same, but perhaps wisely decided that no paper more striking than the bucrania themselves should be used. An interesting analysis by Professor Pace of the layers of paint overlying these plaster heads reveal that their original color was "a light creamy beige."[16] The walls may have been painted in the same color; certainly there is no trace of paper from the 1830 period. A Victorian photograph (fig. 49) shows walls of a natural wood color upon which has been painted a rather simple but three dimensional pattern of arches supporting medallions of some

A

B

48.
Estouteville: (a) *white and gilt china basket with scalloped dishes, 1835;* (b) *an astral lamp (shade replaced) on Empire table; from a pair bought in Philadelphia in 1835, for Estouteville hall. (Photo by Edwin S. Roseberry from a private collection.)*

49.
Estouteville: great hall as it appeared in the Victorian era, showing a reddish-brown frieze with three-dimensional design painted on walls. (Photo courtesy Valentine Museum, Richmond, Va.)

kind. The color used corresponds to layer four, the reddish brown described in Professor Pace's analysis. As Selina herself did not die until 1870, it is possible that this later treatment conformed to her taste, although it was certainly influenced by the Victorian ideas of the new generation. Today we might find the effect of these painted walls pleasing, if a little dark.

Very typical features of this Victorian hall are the deer head and the stuffed fox mounted above the doors. They were no doubt the fruit of the chase, brought down by John's son Peyton. This son had been instructed by his father: You must be the best at whatever you choose to do: farming or fox hunting. Peyton chose fox hunting. There were books at Estouteville, but it is not certain that Peyton read them. There is a faint echo here of the sentiments of an anonymous sixteenth-century gentleman quoted by Mark Girouard in his *Life in the English Country House*: "It becomes the sons of gentlemen to blow the horn nicely [he meant the hunting horn], to hunt skilfully and elegantly, to carry and train a hawk. But the study of letters should be left to the sons of rustics."[17]

Also visible in this invaluable Victorian photograph is the Jarvis portrait of Isaac. (See fig. 57.) John III's son Peyton had followed the all-too-prevalent Virginia custom of marrying his first cousin, Isaac's daughter Isaetta. The portrait must have come to Isaetta, possibly after her mother's death in 1876.

Portraits, in fact, play a most important role in Coles family life. To return to the earlier experience of Helen in Philadelphia in 1835, we have a vivid description of her visits to the studio of Mr. Sully. Thomas Sully, 1783–1872, was at the time Philadelphia's acknowledged master. He was a native of England and had come to America at the age of nine, returning to England to study briefly under Benjamin West. Helen closes one of her frequent letters to Selina: "Farewell—my time has come to go to the painting room."[18] It would appear that the sittings in the painting room were not a chore, but occasions enjoyed by both artist and patrons. Helen described Sully at work: "He is remarkably good natured—pleasant in conversation, and encourages his sitters to tell him freely of their objections to his work; but his own native politeness will always operate against its being done without due regard to his feelings. His is without doubt a master's touch—and should be at such prices. Our two, though only to the waist, will cost without frames $250, and complete, not much short of $300." At a special show at Sully and Earle's Gallery of Paintings on Chestnut Street, the portraits of Tucker (fig. 50) and Helen (fig. 51) were a great success. Helen is serene and beautiful beneath her plumed hat. "Mr. Short avers that Raphael himself could not have succeeded better."

> 'tis said that Sully is proud of his execution in mine, and very desirous to have it seen. He told me that the style of dress was the best that he had ever painted, simple yet beautiful,—in truth, said he, 'Tis a pleasure, not a trouble, to paint it. [Helen had her reservations about the costume.] . . . 'Tis to be hoped that Mrs. Pinhard will consent to exchange or take back the Spanish hat and feathers in which my portrait is taken, for it will be useless to me afterwards. . . . I told him . . . that the Lady he was providing for me certainly had not the habit of staying all day in the garden—with her Bonnet over her arm—as the original did. . . . He seemed to think that he had the privilege of making the picture as handsome as he could so long as the likeness was preserved.[19]

In this case, at least, Sully had not had to strain the truth of his vision, for Helen was indeed a beautiful woman. The likeness, she insisted, was too genteel looking, "especially after a bout of gardening and rock picking, etc." However, it was an "interesting *picture*."[20]

50.
Tucker Coles of Tallwood, 1782–1861, oil on canvas, by Thomas Sully, 1835. (Photo courtesy Francis Jenks and the Frick Art Reference Library.)

51.
Helen Skipwith Coles (Mrs. Tucker Coles), 1789–1864, of Tallwood, oil on canvas, by Thomas Sully, 1835. (Photo courtesy Francis Jenks and the Frick Art Reference Library.)

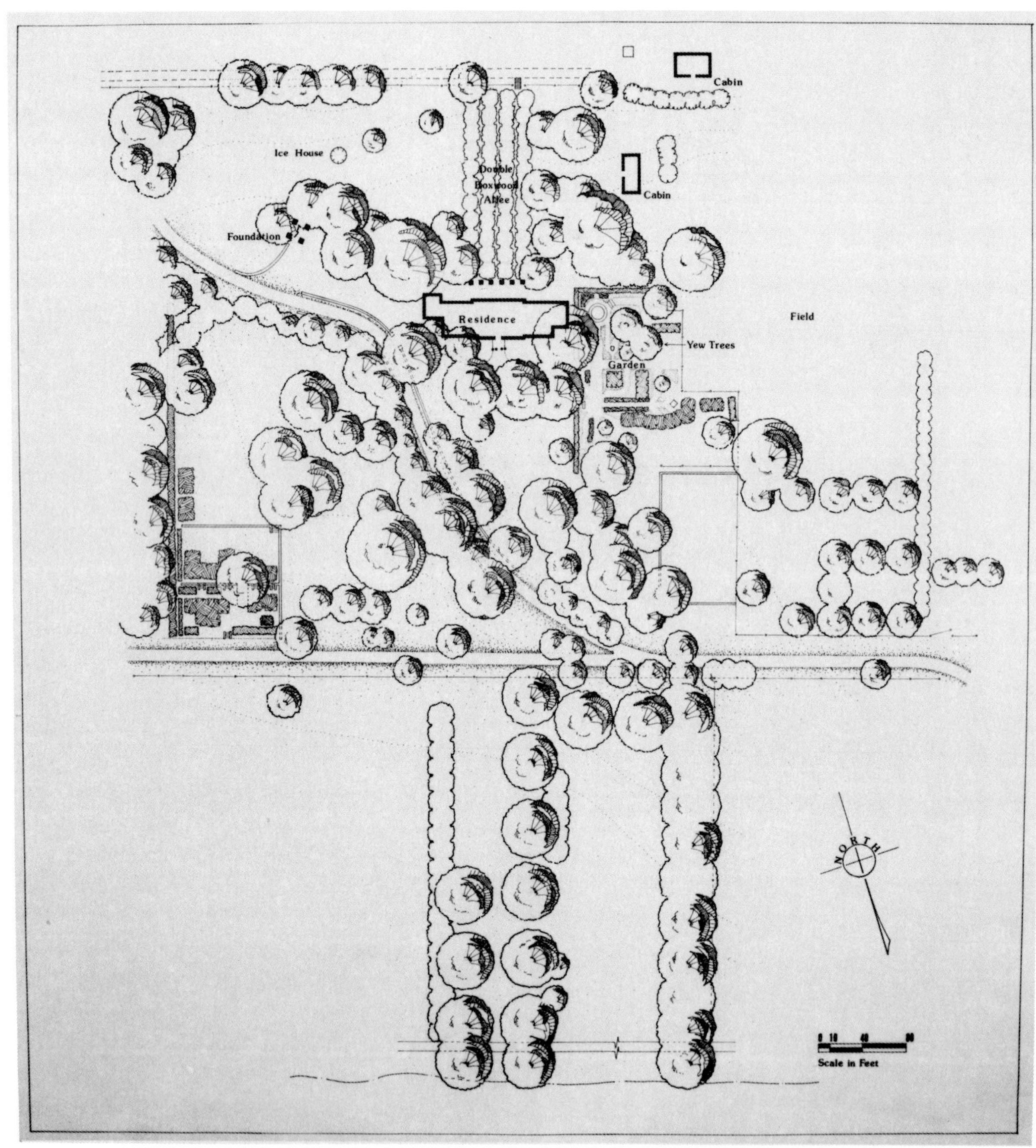
Cabin
Ice House
Double Boxwood Allee
Cabin
Foundation
Residence
Field
Yew Trees
Garden
NORTH
Scale in Feet

52.
Tallwood, site plan. Much of the existing site organization dates from the tenure of the Chauvenet famiy in the 1920s and 1930s. Helen's garden, to the east of the house, preserves traces of the original rectilinear design. The yew trees no longer form a room. (Drawn by Patricia A. Fiedler, 1984, based on field survey by Cynthia Fink, Bryan Katen, and Foster Paulette, under the supervision of William D. Rieley.)

GARDENS

The reference to "gardening and rock picking" would seem to suggest that Helen had done some of that work with her own hands. Both girls had before them the example of their mother; Lady Skipwith's garden at Prestwould rivaled, if it did not surpass, the great gardens of her day. The daughters' gardens (see figs. 52, 53) were laid out in the same old-fashioned squares, bisected by paths. Following the parental examples at Prestwould and Enniscorthy, both were placed east of the house. The one at Estouteville is slightly canted in relation to the house, a deviation from the norm perhaps accounted for by the planting in connection with the earlier house. Previously established roads may also have influenced the siting of the garden.

Letters in Jefferson's *Farm Book* refer to gifts of Mayduke cherries and the famous pear trees from Enniscorthy and Woodville. From the earliest years the Coles were noted for their fruit trees and for the profusion of flowers in their gardens. At Tallwood "the air was heavy with damask roses, and the sweet briar hedge in full bloom. In Helen's 'English Square' the roses were all so tender that barrels had to be placed over them to protect them in winter." The roses, of course, were part of Helen's English (or Scottish) heritage, passed on directly from her mother. Another import was the yew trees, famous at Tallwood and virtually a Coles garden trademark. Other flowers referred to in letters were "fiery lillies," martigons (a species of Turk's cap), mock orange, crape myrtle, flowering almond, a Carolina Syringa with blossoms as large as dogwood—but not fragrant—magnolias, scarpian senna, and a vine called busy-bodies. When Helen saw the first flowering of her nasturtium, she thought it "so incomparably the most beautiful of blossoms that I dared not pluck it."[21]

In Tallwood's garden the unique feature, now lost, was the ancient yew trees, grown together to form a spacious outdoor room. The light filtering through their dense crowns was dim, subterranean. In this private place no sound penetrated but the murmur of bees overhead. The yews marked one edge of her garden, the wilder part, where yellow jessamine and the rich blossoming crape myrtle grew. On terraces falling away to the east of the formal squares, both Helen and Selina grew their abundant fruits: strawberries, gooseberries, cherries, peaches, pears and plums, grapes and melons, apricots, nectarines, celestial figs (brought up from Prestwould; a fig tree still volunteers on the edge of Selina's garden—see fig. 54). There were also nuts: Spanish chestnuts, English walnuts, and almonds. These last were particularly valued for their contribution to desert. At Estouteville

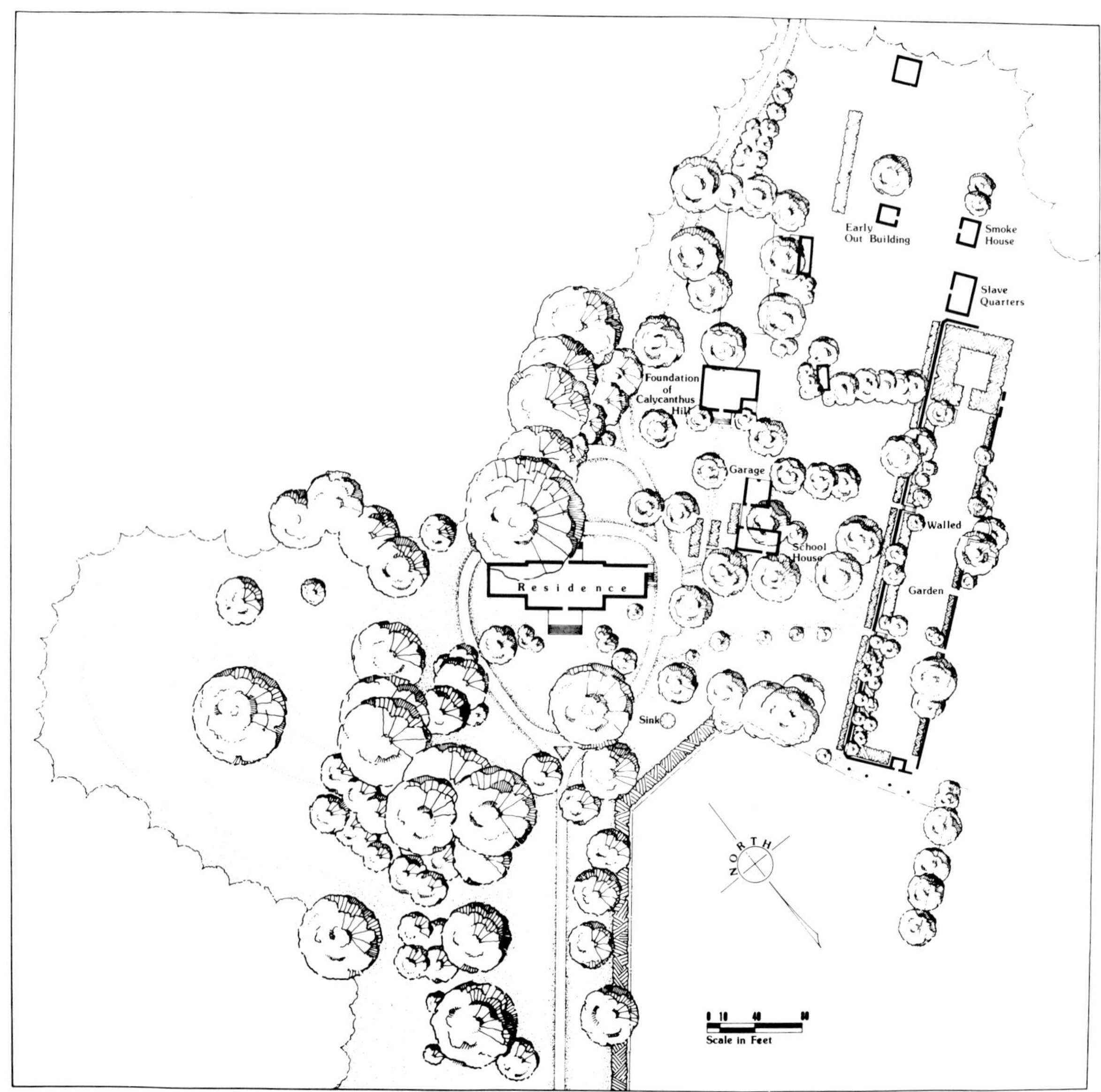

calycanthus still grew down both sides of the drive, for native plants were as much a part of the scene as the imported roses. In this too the girls were following their mother's example.

In addition to the native flowers there was a profusion of edible plants to be domesticated by the careful gardener. Berries and grapes grew in great variety, the grapes in bunches so heavy that they weighed down their branches, only waiting to be trained on arbors. One made persimmon beer, peach and apple brandy. That Jefferson, 1809, could list thirty-nine varieties of vegetables growing in the garden at Monticello shows in what profusion they could be grown in that fertile

53.
Estouteville. This site plan shows the house, the garden site to the east, and the foundations of a late-eighteenth-century dwelling, Calycanthus Hill. The slave quarters date from this period or earlier, and the elegant brick smokehouse from c. 1830. The terraces below the garden were planted in fruit trees. The house is surrounded by the original grove of magnificent tulip poplars. (Drawn by Patricia A. Fiedler, 1984, under the supervision of William D. Rieley; field survey by Cynthia Fink, Bryan Katen, and Foster Paulette.)

54.
Estouteville, entrance to the garden, c. 1930. (Photo by Frances Benjamin Johnson, 1930s, Library of Congress.)

soil.[22] In 1705 Robert Beverly wrote "The Kitchen Garden don't come any finer than the ones we have in Virginia."[23]

There was no lack of the necessary outbuildings: at Tallwood many have disappeared but they appear in old photographs and can be located on the site plan. At Estouteville an especially handsome brick smokehouse and very early slave quarters remain in the yard (fig. 55a, b). A "necessary house," no longer standing, was just outside the garden wall.

In all the houses both sanitation and heating remained simple—depending on the dressing stand with washbowl and chamber pot for the one and on the open fireplace for the other. The expertly designed Rumford fireplace of 1796—which narrowed the throat of the chimney, reduced the size of the fireplace opening, and placed it between inclined walls of brick—did help, but the universal use of embroidered fire screens to shield the face shows that the heat produced was too concentrated for comfort.

Kitchen smells and noises were kept at a distance, very often, particularly in the earlier buildings, they were under a separate roof.

A

B

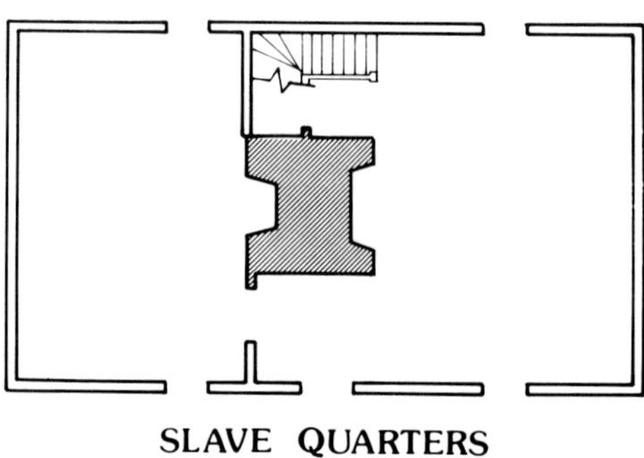

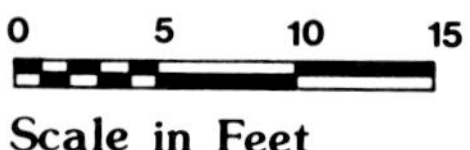

55.
Estouteville, slave quarters and smokehouse. (Photo [a] *courtesy Stevens & Company; measured drawing* [b] *by Patricia A. Fiedler, 1984.)*

At Enniscorthy, Estouteville, and Tallwood they occupied the commodious cellars. Hot water was sometimes used under serving dishes, but even with the dumbwaiter at Estouteville one does not imagine that the dishes always arrived hot. It was, of course, the numerous servants that made existence comfortable, and that perhaps tended to make a more advanced technology appear superfluous. Jefferson at Monticello and Robert Carter at Redlands employed rather simple contrivances for at least removing, if not emptying, the ever-present chamber pots. At Redlands a shaft from an upper floor to the cellar conveyed the necessary article by a sort of dumbwaiter. The idea may have been suggested to both men by their experience in England, where such refinements had long existed.

Ice was supplied fairly effectively by blocks cut in winter from the farm pond, which were packed in straw and stored in an underground icehouse (see fig. 52). There is an amusing letter from Ellen Wayles Randolph, who was staying with her Grandfather Jefferson at Poplar Forest in 1819. He had insisted that they use a newfangled appliance, "which he called a refrigerator." It resulted in butter that ran around the plate, and wine that remained at room temperature. During this introduction to a new age, Burwell, the butler, had been ill. Upon his return to his post, the butter too returned to its normal habitat in a plain box packed in snow.[24]

Meats were usually smoked or salted for preservation. Southern hospitality, it has been pointed out, was built on the presence of that famous and dependable delicacy the Virginia ham. Even though messages were frequently carried great distances by family, friends, or trusted slaves, there were few occasions when the housewife could be sure who or how many would turn up for dinner or the night. This is where the indispensable ham came into play. Hospitality was offered, not to friends or acquaintances alone, but to the passing wayfarer. This was true to a very late date in these country areas. A reminiscence of Estouteville in the nineties recalls one such character: when offered a second helping of ham he replied politely, "No, thankee kindly. I'll make do with this butter." At the close of the meal he asked his host what he might owe for the entertainment. When assured that he owed nothing, he responded with heartfelt regret, "If I'd a knowed it, I'd a et more ham!"[25]

The garden, of course, was another ever-ready source of refreshment in season. At Prestwould orange trees raised in the greenhouse were stood in pots in the upstairs hall in winter, and we know that Estouteville too had its greenhouse. It was built on the foundations of the old Calycanthus Hill, and supplied the hospital in Charlottesville during the Civil War. At Tallwood we may call it Helen's garden, but Tucker too was an horticultural expert. We read of him playing host to a horticultural tour where one guest, Mrs. Cocke of Bremo, was so impressed that her husband wrote a friend that she had not been out of the garden all day.[26]

Tucker, of course, was also interested in the medicinal aspects of his garden. We may remember that his mother-in-law Skipwith had left him her domestic medicine chest (by Maxwell), and there was also Dr. Ewell's book of home remedies grown in the garden. The famous Dr. Physic himself was not above prescribing an astringent of partly ripe persimmons, a poultice of roast turnip, and a concoction of red rose leaves (use unknown). Lady Skipwith may not have visited Tucker's garden, but he certainly visited hers, where unquestionably they discussed horticultural matters, particularly those of a medicinal nature.

The fruits of the garden came to the table in many and various forms, especially on occasions such as the visit of James and Cousin Dolley Madison to Enniscorthy. Helen wrote a lively account:

> You would have supposed that all the good things of life "came of themselves". . . . we sat down to dinner drest in our best, and looking as though we had never thought of anything more plebean than simply to taste the various delicacies placed before us; tho in truth the suggesting and preparing them had afforded us (Brother Isaac at the head) no little diversion. [As the guests arrived] Mrs. Madison and Mrs. T. M. Randolph who accompanied her greeted Mama like daughters. . . . Mrs. Madison kissed me, protesting she had known me long and intimately. . . . However her singularly majestick and striking appearance may awe one at first, yet her sweetly conciliating manner never fails to place you perfectly at ease. . . . The President is a very ordinary looking little gentleman. . . . but his looks are far from doing justice to his powers of entertaining, and he is truly a witty and pleasant little man.[27]

Such a dinner was customarily served by placing a variety of dishes on the table, which was later cleared for the dessert course. It was usually a great deal less formal, even at the president's house in Washington, than the famous twenty-seven course dinner at Prestwould. When the Madisons were entertained at Enniscorthy the company enjoyed hams, "drest" with "salats" and every good thing, nor did Madison have to tell his risqué stories on water alone.

At some point during the entertainment the guests may have admired the deer park, one of the refinements of English landscaping to be found at both Enniscorthy and Monticello. The new furniture and the gardens all spoke well of the Coles's economy. The land may have been declining in productivity, but then there was plenty of it. There was wheat as well as the old staple crop of tobacco. Tucker

Coles's account book for 1833–34 survives in the family's possession and shows a large volume of business at his mill. After John II's death we have no regular itemized lists of expenditures, but John III kept an overall record that we have already consulted in regard to his building expenses and where he also recorded expenses for furnishing.

In 1830, the year of the completion of the fine new house, $3,416.05 appears under the heading purchase of furniture. This was about three-quarters of the year's profit from the plantation: $4,519.08. Not surprisingly, it resulted in a $1,215 deficit at the end of the year, still not an excessive figure for a man whose assets were assessed at the time at $90,000. Tucker's worth at this time was assessed at half that amount. The Coles, of course, were busy consolidating their position as members of the upper gentry. After the breakup of John II's estate they no longer met Heather Clemenson's definition (as applied in nineteenth-century Great Britain) of a great landowner as one "possessing a minimum of 10,000 acres,"[28] but by the 1830s in Virginia land was no longer the sole criterion of wealth, much less of status.

Andrew Stevenson, for example, possessed very little real property, but as Speaker of the House in Washington he enjoyed both political status and social eminence. In October of 1833 Joseph Cabell described a dinner party at Estouteville where "Speaker Stevenson arouses even his cautious brothers-in-law in favor of Improvements for the Western Country."[29] Stevenson's advice was followed, for at the time of his death in 1861 Tucker Coles owned stock in the James River and Kanawha Company and in the Staunton and James River Turnpike Company. No railroad stock appears in the record of his estate.[30] From the first incorporation (1818) of the town of Scottsville, the Coles brothers had owned a large share (fifteen acres) of the newly laid out lots. Like virtually all their fellow citizens in Albemarle, they were wedded to the system of river-canal traffic, and like Scottsville itself, they missed the great future portent of the railroad. But all that lay ahead. For the present, that is to say in the early thirties, they were quite content with things as they were.

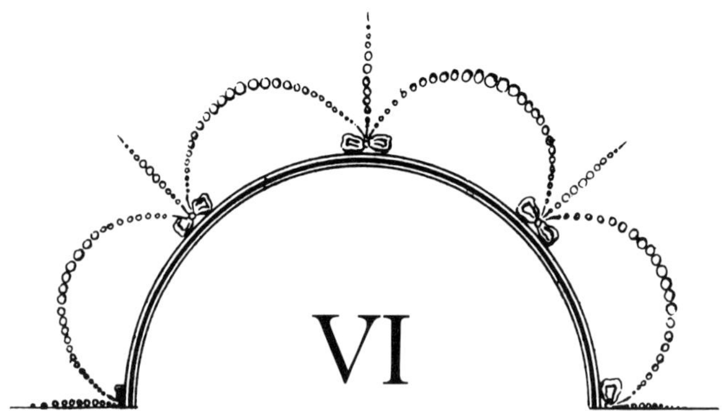

VI

Isaac, 1780–1841

No one could have anticipated the decade of the 1830s with more genuine and well-justified enthusiasm than the heir to Enniscorthy. For so long Isaac's position had been an anomalous one. Although Thomas Jefferson had effected the repeal of the old law of primogeniture, older sons were still commonly among the large landholders, set up on plantations of their own. We have seen it happen in the Coles family with Walter and John. Isaac had to wait for his inheritance. Under his father's will he inherited 1,250 acres of Enniscorthy outright; the house and an additional 1,000 acres were subject to the life interest of his mother. These two generous and amiable temperaments should have been able to get along together, but significantly the heir never settled down at Enniscorthy for any length of time during his mother's lifetime. There was a generation gap, a difference of view on the way returns from the farm should be spent.

Isaac, as much a son of his forward-looking employer, Mr. Jefferson, as of his own conservative parent, leaned toward what he described as the comforts as opposed to the necessaries of existence. He bought wine, he bought himself a gig. For one so much on the road as Isaac, this last was perhaps no extravagance. When he farmed, he wanted to do so in the latest and best way, and he was not afraid of capital investment. Isaac considered these improvements, and other matters, in a series of letters to his great friend and contemporary Joseph C. Cabell of Nelson County.

These two young men had probably known each other since childhood, for at least one Cabell child had stayed at Enniscorthy to take advantage of the presence of a tutor there,[1] and the families, of course, knew each other well. Cabell was about a year older than Isaac Coles, and was not more than a year ahead of him when both attended the College of William and Mary. Cabell spent nearly four years in Paris (1802–6), and Isaac was in Paris in 1804, so that their paths again crossed.

Their wholly delightful correspondence begins before Cabell's departure for France. Both were as yet unsettled in life; they were younger sons, each about to inherit land without an accompaning house or settled base. Isaac's first letter of January 1802 exhorts his friend: "I pray you Cabell not to give way to that melancholy in which of late you have but too much indulged.... A similar turn of mind has frequently of itself given me a degree of fever."[2] In Isaac's case a series of apparently hopeless love affairs could easily have accounted for his feverish state of mind. His Parisian tour obviously effected a cure, for the next "fever" of which he tells his friend is caused by a beautiful *fille de chambre*, "who was withall a most egregious coquetta." Egregious or not, this beautiful chambermaid seems to have had no trouble in putting off the young man from America. "I made love to her and thought myself most fortunate. She promised to be kind and kept me for two whole nights shaking and trembling at every sound that passed along the gallery, but Leonora did not come."[3]

Cabell, more fortunate in love, and perhaps more genuinely disposed toward settling down, was married in 1807 to Mary Walker Carter, heiress to a large part of the old Carter estate of Corotoman. His letters to his friend extol the charms of matrimony. Isaac meanwhile had taken on a most interesting job; he was private secretary to Mr. Jefferson, then in his second term as president of the United States. It was at this time that Isaac referred to "H.[elen] S.[kipwith]" and her "august parent." His experience in Washington had taught him "that in the great world they only are successful in the field of Venus who wield a golden spear. Mine, you know, has not even a gilded point."[4]

His position as private secretary was a confidential one. As earlier described by Jefferson himself, it was "more that of an *aide de camp* than that of a mere secretary."[5] He was in a position to pass on to Cabell many interesting aspects of the president's foreign policy and of the country's delicate position between the two great warring powers, Britain and France. "I no longer have any idea that we will have war. We might have it indeed with England.... or with France.... It would be as little our policy to be drawn into the vortex of their quarrels as it would be our interest that the one or the other should be destroyed, a greater misfortune could not befall this country than to see united in the same hands the dominion of the sea and of the land." There was, of course, the continuing danger to American shipping so long as the two great European powers were at war. The president had placed hope in the embargo, suspending all American shipments to England or France, "an experiment," Isaac wrote, "which I wish much to see made, for if it is indeed the powerful weapon which we have been taught to believe we shall never again have occasion to use it."[6] In which belief both Isaac and the president were sadly overconfident.

Personal matters too were engaging the attention of these two young men. Should Cabell settle on his wife's Corotoman property in the Tidewater, or should he remain at Edgewood, and build on his own Nelson County land? John II's death in 1808 had caused Isaac to make a close analysis of his own position on an up-country plantation. At the same time his sketch of the comforts of a Tidewater establishment point to future ambitions of his own.

> the chief profit from one of these large tidewater estates is not so much the revenue which they yield, as the comfort which they afford to the actual residents. A large family might be supported at Corotoman; your table might every day in the year be laden with delicacies; you might entertain the large circle of your friends in the most sumptuous manner. . . .
>
> As to the particular advantages of yours [Edgewood], my own impression is that they are solely to the actual occupants, and that the estate loses half its value to any other. I will prove it to you in a dozen words. The crop on the Green Mountain this year is supposed to be an average one, and will give me per hand $140—that is, for each man, woman and plough boy employed in the field. Now according to this calculation, supposing that there are at Corotoman 80 labourers, the crop revenue should be $11,200. It would be this if they were placed on good lands in our country, and were only tolerably managed; and such land could be bought for less money than the Corotoman lands would command.[7]

Isaac was working Enniscorthy with thirteen slaves of his own and eighteen of his mother's, yielding in 1809 the not small return of $4,340 for the year's work, and this in a year when the ups and downs of an expiring embargo would still have been affecting prices. His conclusion, in either case, would appear to be that whether in the Tidewater or on an up-country plantation, the yield would be greatest to a *resident* owner.

At the close of Jefferson's second term Isaac's time in Washington came to an end. One could not spend nearly four years with Mr. Jefferson without acquiring some zeal for improvements and for public service. In Isaac's case such zeal was turned toward Enniscorthy. In 1811 he was writing enthusiastically to Cabell about his fishpond. The pond "comes on charmingly. . . . It will be large enough to furnish me with three hundred and sixty five dishes for my table in the year. . . . It will not be as good as the one at Corotoman, to be sure, but here

56.
Enniscorthy: barn built by Isaac Coles, 1815. (Photo by K. Edward Lay.)

among the wild mountains it cannot but be considered as a vast acquisition. I shall feel happy indeed, if I may contribute by my example to the introduction of little improvements of this sort."[8] He may have already established a deer park, for only three years later we find him supplying Monticello itself with a buck and a doe.[9]

Although his mother would have liked him to settle at Enniscorthy in her lifetime, he never did so for any length of time. When war came in 1812 he wrote to Cabell: "I shall return to Washington to take upon myself the active duties of an officer," delaying even longer the role of the planter. In the next year he even wishes to sell his interest in the estate. Cabell is strenuously opposed: he praises the park at Enniscorthy and refers to the prints in the parlor that he remembered from their days in Paris together. When the sale fails, we find Isaac turning to another solution. "I have some expectation of buying out my mother's life interest. . . . Immediate profit is always the interest of the tenant for life, improvements therefore which will cost money or much labour cannot be expected of one."[10]

This expectation failed, for Rebecca was not convinced. Even so Isaac, entered with enthusiasm into improvements on his own part of the land, some of which may be seen on today's Enniscorthy. His barn, stable, and prize house were nearly complete. A prize house, for those not familiar with the culture of tobacco, might be called a packing shed, a place were tobacco was tamped tightly into hogsheads for shipping down the river. The barn (fig. 56), still in use today, is a fine example of period building. Obviously, Isaac had not spared expense. There are fine details in the beaded siding, unusual in a barn, and box cornices that show where the great rafters fit into notched beams. The windows are fitted with diagonally set wooden louvers. The main floor was used for threshing wheat, which went through a grating to a treadmill on the floor below. Flour was one of Isaac's staple products, along with corn and tobacco. It is interesting to note that he regularly obtained better prices than his neighbor at Monticello. In 1819, for example, Isaac sold tobacco at $11 a hundredweight compared to Jefferson's $5. In 1816 Isaac was getting $5 a barrel for corn, Jefferson somewhat less.[11] Pricing, particularly of tobacco, seems to have been quite arbitrary, but there is little doubt that the Coles were propspering, at a time when Jefferson was constantly going into debt.

In the following year, 1816, Isaac again offered his share of the Enniscorthy estate for sale, at $44,000 for land and improvements, with expectation of realizing another $10,000 or $12,000 from the sale of his Negroes and other personal property. The sale, however, failed to materialize. It was not until the depression of 1819 that Isaac made a major move. Without selling any of his Enniscorthy interest, he went west and made a considerable investment in Missouri land.

In 1823 a brief marriage to Louisa Nevison of Norfolk may have raised hopes of the heir settling permanently at Enniscorthy, but it did not happen. Perhaps there was not time, for Louisa died in the fall of the following year. Even Rebecca's death in 1826 was not the occasion for anchoring Isaac at last. Now a widower, he was once again visiting the northern cities, sometimes in company with his bachelor brother, Edward. Their sister Sally Stevenson, herself living in Washington at this time, remarked that age seemed to have increased the popularity of these two no-longer-youthful beaux. It was from one of these northern visits that Isaac at last brought home the lady who was to succeed Rebecca as mistress of Enniscorthy. His marriage in 1830 was to Julianna Stricker Rankin, widow of the Hon. Christopher Rankin, congressman from Mississippi.

The groom was then fifty years old, yet still handsome, and certainly an attractive man. His portrait by John Wesley Jarvis (fig. 57) shows him in the prime of life; it was probably painted in 1825. At that date Jarvis was in Richmond, painting the portraits, among others, of Mr. and Mrs. William Cabell. Isaac, between marriages and with two sisters in Richmond, was also often seen there. Nothing was more likely than that he should have followed the example of his Cabell friends. With this portrait of Isaac, Jarvis has caught a fine likeness.

57.
Isaac A. Coles, 1780–1841, oil on canvas by John Wesley Jarvis, c. 1825. (Photo by James Abbott, 1982.)

The forehead is highlighted, a Jarvis trademark; the face is sensitive yet strong.

Julianna brought with her to Enniscorthy two additional portraits, by Bass Otis, one of herself (fig. 58) and one of her first husband, the Hon. Christopher Rankin. The portrait of Julianna shows the calm intelligence and poise of his sitter. In that federal society the widow Rankin was a much-sought-after lady. Daniel Webster was a suitor, but although she would admit nothing of the kind, she was already committed to that handsome, if quieter, country gentleman, Isaac Coles. Her portrait by Otis is of enduring value, if not quite as accomplished as the one of her husband by Jarvis. Whether the portrait, done earlier, of the young Louisa Nevison by Cephus Thompson and the one of the late Hon. Christopher Rankin by Otis both hung on Enniscorthy walls, we are not now in a position to tell. Both survived in family hands.

Old Enniscorthy was now to have its late flowering, a final burst of glory in the last decade of Isaac's life. Martha Jefferson Randolph had summed up the situation in a sharp comment made at the time of Isaac's first marriage. "Col. Isaac is said to have married an heiress.... The Coles family are still rising in the world, nor do they appear to have reached the top of the wheel yet, whether they will be exceptions to the general course of nature in private families as in Empires remains to be seen."[12] Which is, in fact, part of the fascination of their story.

Isaac was at last to fulfill his role of builder. He would have a mansion not inferior to anything the Tidewater could show. Enniscorthy II, we recall, was a large two-story frame I-house with wings and a piazza. Isaac set to work at once, and, as we can well imagine, he worked on the grand scale. Cabell was also enlarging Edgewood at this period, and the Coles letters are full of detail interesting to them both. First of all Isaac pulled down 150 feet of his cellar walls—the whole of the central block or core of the old house, whose underpinning may have been too crude for the present builder. It was replaced in 1831 with five-course American with Flemish brick bond, still to be seen in the cellar walls of the present house. This story we must leave for a later chapter.

In October of 1831 Isaac was writing to Cabell: "I have never been so busy in my life. I have made such a change in my old place that you will hardly know it again." In the style he had once described to Cabell, the house should be big enough to entertain a large circle of friends in the most sumptuous manner. To the wings he added pinions and double pinions; the front elevation could not have been less than two hundred

58.
Julianna Stricker Coles (Mrs. Isaac A. Coles) 1796–1876, oil on canvas by Bass Otis, c. 1825. (Photo by James Abbott, 1982.)

feet in length. The new hearths were to be of soapstone at eight dollars a fireplaçe; Isaac complained that "Lewis (the plasterer) . . . did that part of his work so badly that I refused to receive it, and have suspended the payment until Mr. Philips passes upon it."[13]

William B. Phillips, one of Jefferson's workmen, had just finished the brickwork at Estouteville, and was currently working at the little church going up near Dyer's Old Store at Plain Dealing. Isaac was naturally in touch with John and Tucker, and their experienced builders. His house could not be in the Jeffersonian style, but it is significant that he was using Jefferson's workmen. Most striking of all was his use of Burwell, the first slave mentioned in Jefferson's will: "I give to my good, affectionate, and faithful servant Burwell his freedom, and the sum of three hundred dollars, to buy necessaries to commence his trade of glazier, or to use otherwise, as he pleases."[14]

A letter from the overseer Edmund Bacon to Jefferson in 1809 shows that Burwell was painting on top of the house at Monticello at that time, and that he well understood how to mix paints. Bacon's letter quotes Burwell: "He says he has used 300 lbs. of white lead. . . . and that he did not give one coat. He also says that he will need 50 to 100 lbs. dry lead. Burrill [Bacon's phonetic spelling] says it will take 60 gal. of oil."[15] Jefferson followed these instructions by ordering the required linseed oil and dry white lead from Taggert in Philadelphia.

Isaac was buying Wetherell's white lead from the Ellicott Brothers in Baltimore, although, as he told Cabell, it could be ordered through a Richmond agent. He had bought 1,500 pounds in 100-pound kegs, at from nine to eleven cents a pound. Cabell would probably have to pay more, as the price of lead has gone up considerably. Isaac has "left an order with Garland's Store [in North Garden] for a barrel of oil to be filled as opportunity offers. This you will have to keep in glass, or calculate on a loss of about a third to a half. [The pigments] which you may require in small quantities, such as chrome, terra de Sienna [?], litharge, Venetian Red, ______ of lead, copal varnish, etc., may be procured on good terms at Scottsville of Dr. Michie."[16]

Isaac applied to Dryden, the painter in Baltimore, for directions. Burwell used Dryden's receipt for green and yellow chrome for the Venetians (blinds) and found it to answer admirably. Other than chrome green for the blinds, we cannot be sure what colors Isaac used for his house. Clearly it was no small undertaking.

As a practical farmer Isaac, like his brothers, did well. From what we can learn of his transactions, he appears to have bought cheap and to have sold high. In 1832 he had been paying an exceptionally good overseer $250 a year, and raised him to $300, his share of a $1,200 return from the farm acquired from his first wife.[17] The overseer class was notoriously poorly paid, although from the accounts left us, they were also notoriously poor managers. Such men, if able, could usually acquire land of their own. Land was cheap; labor, on the other hand, was high. Desiring to buy additional Negroes in 1810 Coles offered Cabell $2,000 for "five stout healthy young men," which he takes to be "rather above the market price. . . . and the seller may be assured that they will always be treated with humanity and kindness."[18] At the estimated return of $140 per year per hand, man, woman and plough boy, this would seem to be no bad bargain.

Such calculation in regard to human beings is shocking to us today, but as part of a system, it was unavoidable. We have no reason to doubt that Isaac was both a humane and a kind master. He could joke with Cabell about the slave who came with only a rope to pick up a valuable ram, but the tone is one of humorous resignation. At the same time there was always that measure of uneasiness. In the last letter of the series Isaac refers to "A report of an intended Negro insurrection in the Garden [not far to the west of Coles land]. The Camp Meeting at Oliver's[?] gave rise to them. What a horrible state of society is ours where ever families are liable to these alarms which will be forever nearby. Is it not enough to make all fly from such a state of society who have the ability?"[19]

Isaac, of course, had put his finger on the dry rot—the fatal stain, as Jefferson put it—at the heart of the plantation system. Slavery could not survive, and yet, given the economy at that time, it could not easily be abandoned.

The pursuit of happiness was not unmarred, but there were compensations. Enniscorthy was now his, just as Isaac had envisioned it. The house stood secure, one would have thought, among its great trees—one of the most commodious in the state. No one could have foreseen how brief that happiness was to be.

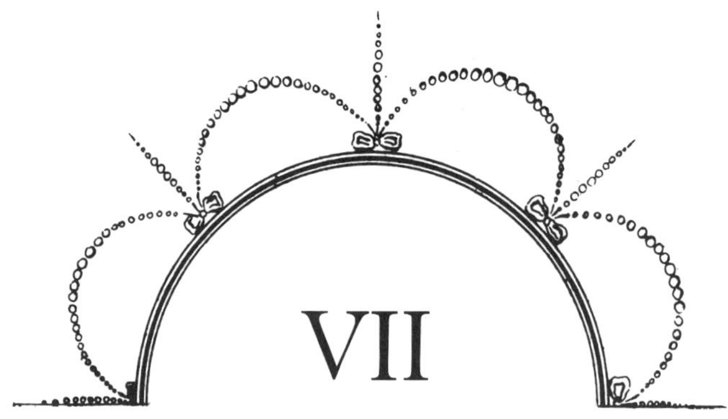

VII

Christ Church, Glendower

Walter, Isaac, Tucker, and John III, all now so well settled in a material way, began at last to turn their attention to more spiritual needs. The official life of the church in St. Anne's Parish had come to an end in 1784. Services had continued to be held from time to time in private homes by such of the clergy who came that way. The Reverend Mr. Hatch, for example, had managed to stop at Monticello for an hour or two in May of 1825, just long enough to marry Ellen Wayles Randolph to Joseph Coolidge. By 1830 a need long felt by south Albemarle for a church and minister of its own was at last about to be met. Old Samuel Dyer, merchant at Plain Dealing, expressed a doubt that sufficient funds could be raised,[1] but John Coles, not surprisingly, surmised that they could.

In 1830, although no church or organized parish then existed in the area, one of John Coles's nephews, Robert Carter of Redlands, went as a delegate to the diocesan meeting at Winchester. On his return, the subsription list was launched. Although the Tucker and John Coles families were the largest contributors, Christ Church, Glendower (fig. 59), was a community project, as the list of sixty-two individual subscribers clearly shows. A rather farther removed but also faithful supporter was General John Hartwell Cocke of Bremo. The Scottsville, Green Mountain, and Carter's Bridge neighborhoods were all represented; there are still families on the original list who worship there today. A committee of three, John Coles, Tucker Coles, and Charles Cocke, let out the building contract, a description of which follows:

59.
Christ Church, Glendower, 1832. (Photo from John S. Wyper, Jr., and Russell C. Scott, "Christ Church Glendower, 1832," Studies in Vernacular Architecture, 1973, under the supervision of K. Edward Lay, typescript, Fiske Kimball Fine Arts Library, University of Virginia.)

An agreement for the erection of the church dated August 23, 1831, was made between Tucker Coles, John Coles, Charles Cocke, agents for the subscribers to the Episcopal church with Walker and Widderfield, Carpenters and House Joiners, by which they agreed to do the woodwork, except the pulpit and window blinds, for $1780; church to be 21 feet high, including the foundations, and 40 by 36 feet from out to out; to have 8 windows with 16 lights of 12″ by 18″—Two ditto over the doors with 12 lights of 12″ by 18″. Two semicircular windows on the [illegible] with Fan Lights; 26 pews in the center without doors and seats with inclined backs in the remaining open under the Gallery and around the altar; a separate bed to be made and raised for the altar and Pulpit; a Gallery across the front of the House over by doors with a flight of stairs of the size and finish of the one now building in the Presbyterian church in Scottsville, the roof to be covered with heart pine shingles with neat Tuscan cornice; the work to be done to keep pace with William B. Phillips the brick layer.[2] [See fig. 60a, b, c.]

60.
Christ Church, Glendower, measured drawings: (a) *front elevation;* (b) *side elevation;* (c) *first-floor plan. (Drawn by Russell C. Scott for John W. Wyper, Jr., and Russell C. Scott, "Christ Church, Glendower, 1832," Studies in Vernacular Architecture, 1973, under the direction of K. Edward Lay, typescript, Fiske Kimball Fine Arts Library, University of Virginia.)*

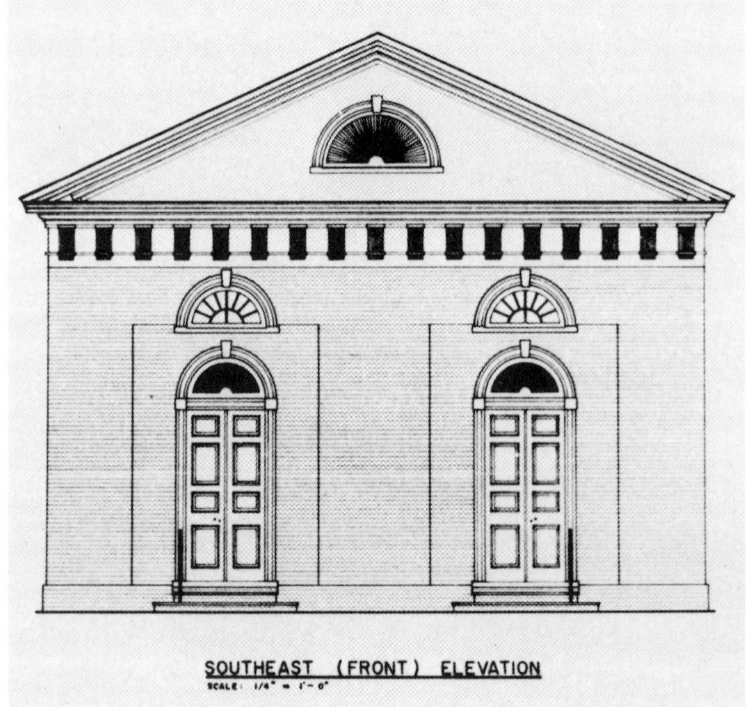

A

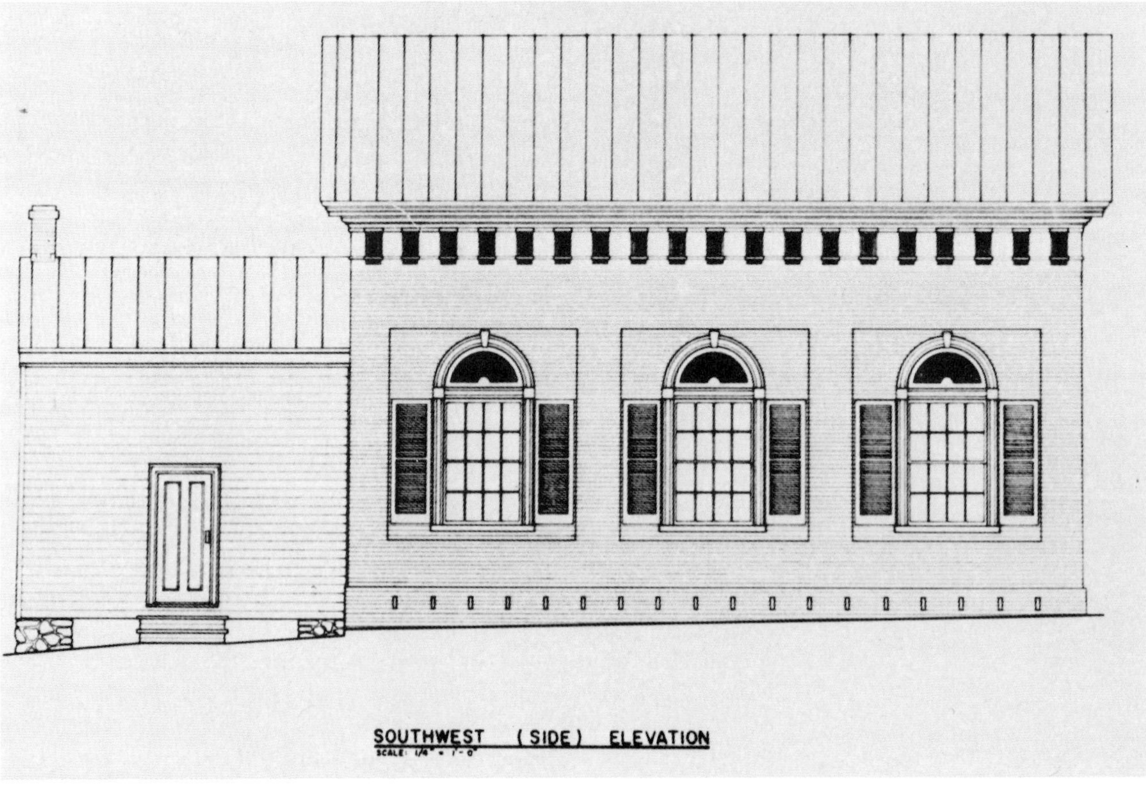

B

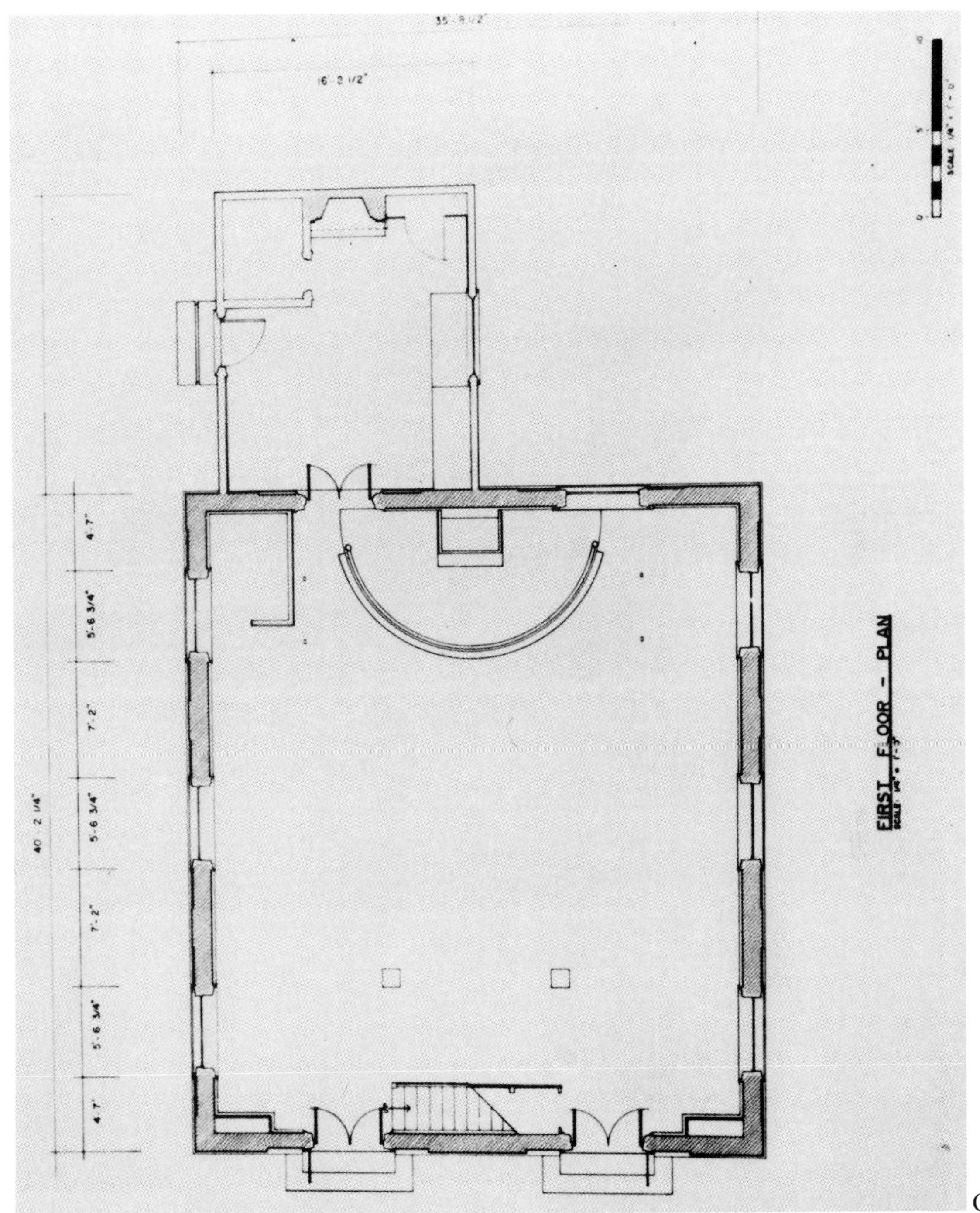

C

A bill for this work was rendered and paid by Tucker Coles, to wit:

Christ Church, Dyer's Store
To acc't. with Tucker Coles Dr.

1832			
Feb. 6	To am't. of Phillips' Bill for brick work		$567.00
Aug.	To am't C. Brown bill for plastering		141.62
1833	To amount of Walker & Widderfield for		
March	woodwork, etc.		1080.00
			$1788.62
Subscription list for Church		1648	
Unpaid		16	1632.00
Amount now due to T. Coles			156.62[3]

An elaborate pulpit and an extremely simple but lovely railing around the chancel were added in 1835. A frame vestry room of no particular quality but happily situated out of sight at the back of the church was added in 1850. There had been no wainscoting or cornice beneath the ceiling in the original plan. These were added during the careful remodeling by the architect Floyd Johnson in 1961. The arrangement of the pews was also altered at this time, substituting one central aisle for the two parallel side aisles of the original plan, a move that reflects the change of emphasis in the worship service from the preaching of the Word to worship at the altar. Two square blocks remaining in the floorboards would seem to indicate that originally the pulpit and the altar had stood each at the head of a side aisle and that one had not been more centrally placed than the other. Indeed, far from being the single focal point, as it now is, the altar had been overshadowed by the much taller pulpit. This elaborate structure, along with the dark-red paint of the walls and other evidences of Victorian taste, have long since disappeared, replaced by light painted walls, white trim, and the simple paneled altar of today.

Although the interior (fig. 61) may thus reflect changes in taste, and even in the character of worship, nothing has changed the beauty of the exterior. To come upon this perfect little building standing alone among its pines, is to experience a shock of pleasure and surprise. Who, or what, may have been responsible, one hundred and fifty years ago, for the perfection of its proportions?

The importance of the contract quoted above may hardly be overestimated, showing, as it does, how a plan may have been arrived at. We know that William B. Phillips was a master brickmason, recently finished with his work at Estouteville, and that he was now employed at Christ Church. James Walker had worked at the university, as had

61.
Christ Church, Glendower: interior, showing altar rail. (Photo from John S. Wyper, Jr., and Russell C. Scott, "Christ Church, Glendower, 1832," Studies in Vernacular Architecture, 1973, under the direction of K. Edward Lay, typescript, Fiske Kimball Fine Arts Library, University of Virginia.)

Widderfield, an apprentice to James Dinsmore, the architect-builder employed by John Coles at Estouteville. The close relationship between the committee and their builders may clearly be seen.

Phillips must also have had in mind the proportions of Jefferson's Christ Church in Charlottesville, built in 1824, for after leaving Glendower he was to build a replica of the Charlottesville building for the Church of St. Thomas in Orange. Another Jeffersonian influence may be seen in the open arrangement of the pews, without the earlier deference to distinctions of class and wealth. There were to be "benches without doors, so that people may be seated without regard to class or condition, pell mell, as they shall lie in death."[4] Very well indeed, although we may doubt that Christ Church members thought of themselves as being buried "pell mell."

In addition to Phillips's experience, which by now would have qualified him as one of the architect-builders of the period, we must not forget that two agents of the vestry charged with the building of the new church had also had considerable building experience of their own. Fanlights, similar to those at Estouteville and Tallwood, are used over the doors of the church. Over the windows the lights were replaced by horizontal louvers. They are particularly effective here, softening the severity of the rectangular walls. The brick walls around doors and windows have been slightly recessed, an Adam-esque touch giving additional relief to the eye. As in any work of art, the effect of simplicity has been won by subtle means. The portico used by Jefferson in his courthouses and at Christ Church Charlottesville has been omitted here—partly, no doubt, to save expense and also because Roman Revival was going out of style.

The vestry desired no imposing Roman temple. In the words of Bishop Meade they were erecting "a neat and excellent brick church"[5] for private worship in a country neighborhood. For one hundred and fifty years it has fulfilled that purpose, serving as the central point for a society of scattered country homes. For generations children have come to Christ Church Glendower, grown to manhood or womanhood, and passed from the scene. Just as the beauty of language of the King James version of the Bible, read Sunday after Sunday, has surely had its effect, so the beauty and fitness of the little building has left its mark on the children of Christ church. Many have been christened, married, and buried here. The erection of this little church in 1832 marks a high point in post-Jeffersonian building in Albemarle.

VIII

The Daughters

With the completion of the little church in the 1830s, we may say that the Coles family building had reached a summit. Estouteville and Tallwood were complete, and Isaac had spared no pains in enlarging John II's Enniscorthy. The family itself had reached a high point on which it appeared to rest. So far we have seen them mainly through the matter-of-fact pages of their account books, or through the rather bland eyes of Helen, who seems not to have resembled in any way her formidable mother. Turning one by one to the daughters of the Coles family, we may get a sharper view.

Mary Elizabeth Coles Carter we may leave at Redlands, doing very well indeed out of her plantation, and investing money through her youngest brother, Edward, in Missouri lands. The history of this brother we shall leave for later, for Edward was indeed a maverick, an untypical member of a typical family. The second daughter, Rebecca, married into the great landowning Singleton family of South Carolina. Old Rebecca had put it neatly in her will: To my daughter Rebecca Singleton "being already possessed of more fortune than is necessary for her own happiness . . . I leave . . . only as a token of my affection for her one of my best damask table clothes and my set of old silver spoons."[1] In other words (and this seems to have been the view held in a mild way by the rest of the family), she already had more money than was good for her. The fact was that there was a difference in life-style between the Virginia Piedmont and the South Carolina plantations, which reflected a difference in their economies. The Coles of Albemarle could and did personally supervise their lands, which was not possible for a landowner such as Richard Singleton, owner of numerous estates. John Coles II and Walter Coles of Woodville had both been noted breeders of thoroughbred horses, but Singleton was a

62.
Phenomena, *oil on canvas by Eduard Troye, c. 1837. (Photo by Edwin S. Roseberry from a private collection.)*

different sort of horseman, a celebrated racing man. As sister Betsy wrote home when she visited the Singletons at their home, Hills of Santee, Richard had no less than seven top horses in training, "the best one for the great race in Virginia next spring."[2] Betsy was not a racing enthusiast.

No Singleton portraits survive, at least not in the Coles connection, but surely the finest of any surviving painting still in Coles family hands is that of the Singleton mare Phenomena, by the master painter of thoroughbreds Eduard Troye (fig. 62). She is royally bred, by Sir Archie out of Lottery; Sir Archie is by the great Diomed and is himself progenitor of the line that produced the greatest of all American thoroughbreds, Man o' War. Richard Singleton chose this painting to

63.
Early portrait of Andrew Stevenson, 1787–1857, oil on canvas by Cephus Thompson, 1810. (Photo by Edwin S. Roseberry, courtesy University of Virginia.)

send to England with his brother-in-law Andrew Stevenson, when Stevenson went as the American minister to the Court of St. James's. The idea was to show those intolerably conceited English that Americans too were capable of breeding fine horseflesh.

BLENHEIM

Which leads us to the next Coles sister, Sarah. Sally had been a longtime favorite of the Madisons. As a young girl she had leaned over the banisters of the Octagon House in Washington, the president's temporary home, crying, "Peace, Peace"; thus Sally announced the end

64.
Sarah Coles Stevenson (Mrs. Andrew Stevenson), 1784–1848, oil on canvas by G. P. A. Healy, 1840. (Photo courtesy of Virginia Historical Society, Richmond.)

of the War of 1812. The president took it calmly, but his maître d'hôtel was drunk for three days. The next year, 1816, Sally married Andrew Stevenson (fig. 63). According to her sister-in-law Helen, Sally was the only one of the Coles girls who was not pretty; she was "witching." Today we would have added a prefix, "*be*witching." The Stevensons had been popular wherever they went, in Richmond and then in Washington, where Stevenson was Speaker of the House in the Jackson administration. In the thirties he was sent to London, where the minister and his wife became the new thing, all the rage in fashionable society.

Sally's portrait by G. P. A. Healy (fig. 64), taken in London, shows her at the height of her powers, and Healy at his accomplished best. It hangs now in the Virginia Historical Society. A companion portrait of her husband was unfortunately severely damaged by fire. The sophisticated lady shown in the Healy portrait did her diplomatic duty without the aid of a secretary: returning innumerable calls and observing all about her with a sharp eye. The Stevensons were in London for the coronation of the young Victoria; this and other occasions were described in vivid detail in the course of her long letters to Virginia. On the American minister's salary Sally had to refurbish her feathers and dye her pelisse, but all the same "I do very well."[3] We may be sure that she did.

The Stevensons returned home in 1841. In 1846 they bought Edward Carter's Blenheim and rebuilt on the old site. The Carter house had burned. The present Blenheim (fig. 65) does not look like the sort of house that the Stevensons would have designed for themselves; it looks somewhat like an extension of something already there, and probably, at the least, foundations and a cellar had remained from the old house built by Edward Carter. The Stevensons erected on this site two single-pile frame sections, the new section placed end to end with the old. It is, in fact, a double house with two porticoes and two entrance doors. The pointed Gothic Revival window frames are obviously a fashionable detail brought by the Stevensons from their time in England. A very simple and elegant single-room building stands detached in the yard, built, it is said, to house Minister Stevenson's library. It plainly was conceived independently, possessing greater classical elegance than the cottage style of the house.

If Sally read much herself, it is not recorded, but while in England she had made a pilgrimage to the scenes of her favorites: to meet Wordsworth in the Lake Country and to visit Sir Walter's Melbourne Abbey—a romantic taste in literature to equal a taste for the Gothic Revival in architecture. We remember that John II had been happy to

65.
New Blenheim, c. 1846: English cottage style. (Photo courtesy Stevens & Company.)

66.
Blenheim, library. (Photo courtesy Stevens & Company.)

67.
Aerial view of Blenheim grounds, showing the garden east of the house. (Photo courtesy Stevens & Company.)

say that his daughters were not learned, but learned or not, Sally was not one moment behind the times. She was also a born writer. Her letters describing the life of London catch all the brilliance and glitter of that society, so different from her own Albemarle.

Unhappily, Sally Coles Stevenson did not live to enjoy her husband's retirement to what they no doubt thought of as the simple rural cottage they were building at Blenheim. They had bought as near to the Green Mountain as possible. In 1846, Richmond, Washington, London were all behind her. She had time to think of her windows and to plan a garden in the approved Coles location, east of the house (see fig. 67), but she was never to occupy the new house. Sally Stevenson died in 1847. Although she never lived there, Blenheim retains the feeling she had planned for herself, of retreat from a busy world.

ROCK CASTLE

On a spring day in 1732, that adventurous man and lively writer William Byrd II had stopped off at Tuckahoe on his way to the mines. He had chided young Tarleton Fleming for lingering in his wife's, Mary Randolph's, comfortable home on the James, when in Byrd's view he should have been building a house for himself on his lands upriver in Goochland County. Fleming took his advice. The site of his new house, called Rock Castle (fig. 68a–b), is magnificent indeed. It stands on a bluff (hence its name) some hundred feet or more above the James. The waters here, already fed by the Hardware and the Rivanna, move majestically downstream. On this level site, great trees—the

A

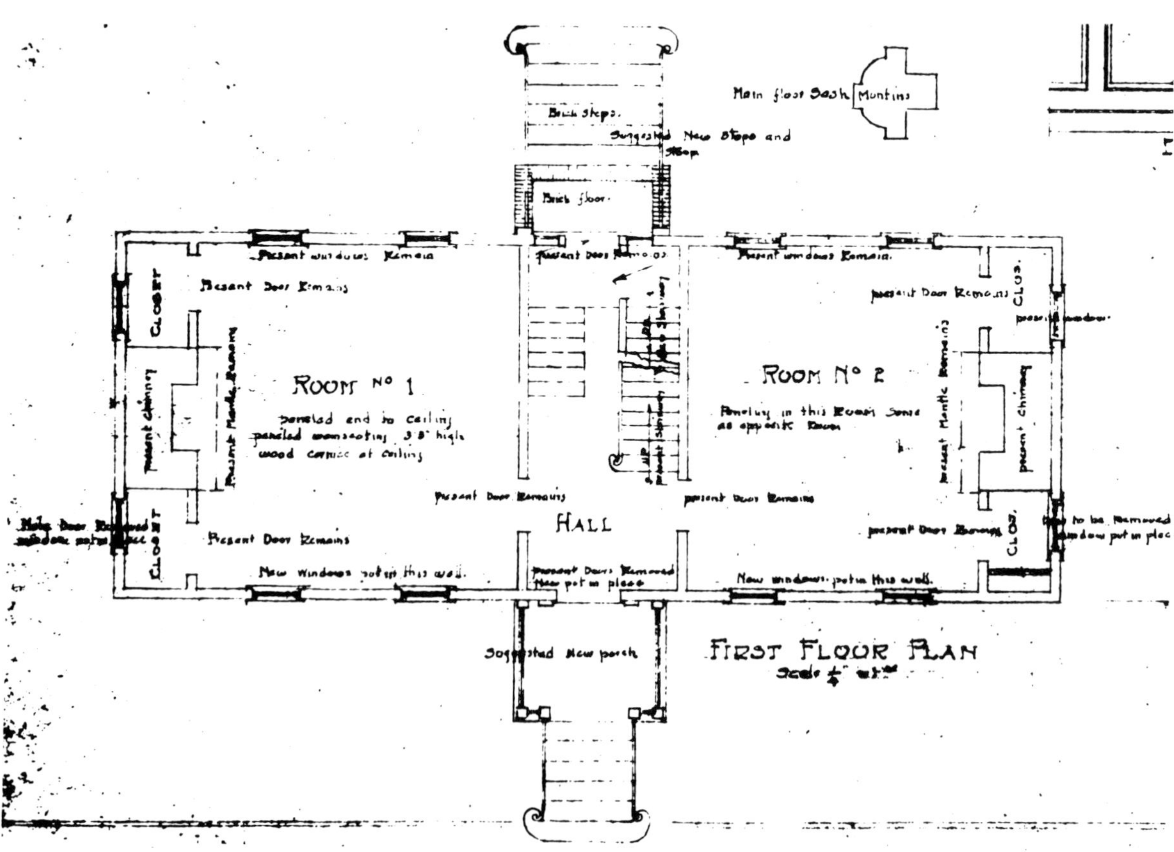
Main floor Sash Muntins
Brick steps.
Suggested New Steps and Stoop
Brick floor
Present windows Remain
Present Door Remains
CLOSET
ROOM No 1
paneled end to ceiling
paneled wainscoting 3.0" high
wood cornice at ceiling
Present chimney
Present Mantle Remains
HALL
ROOM No 2
Paneling in this Room Same as opposite Room
CLOS.
New windows put in this wall.
Present Doors Removed New put in place
Suggested New porch
FIRST FLOOR PLAN

B

68.
Rock Castle, c. 1732. (a) *This 1923 photo shows the early jerkinhead roof, and the portico added by John Coles Rutherfoord, c. 1850;* (b) *first-floor plan. (Photo from James River Garden Club,* Historic Gardens of Virginia *[Richmond: William Byrd Press, 1923], opposite p. 125; drawing courtesy Mrs. Henry Taylor, Taylor and Parrish, General Contractors, Richmond.)*

poplar, the elm, the hickory—rise to as great heights again as the bluff rises above the river. Fleming had built here a frame I-house, a story and a half, one room deep, with chimneys set forward into the rooms beneath the jerkinhead roof typical of an even earlier day. It looks now much as it looked then.

Emily Ann Coles married John Rutherfoord in 1816. The Rutherfoords lived in Richmond, where he became a member and later president of the Council of State and was acting governor in 1841. In 1843 they purchased Rock Castle, their summer home. It became a convenient stopping place for family and visitors between Richmond and the Green Mountain section. Their son, John Coles Rutherfoord, made it his permanent home.

Young Rutherfoord wished to enlarge and to "modernize." Directly in front of the old house he put up a Greek Revival structure, c. 1850, showing Italianate detail, said to be the fruit of Rutherfoord's European tour.[4] Behind this building the old house remained virtually untouched. In 1935 an entirely new house was built on the site, and the later addition was removed. At this time the old eighteenth-century house was moved to a site about a hundred yards back. Here it still stands, a record of a much earlier time.[5]

The interior, too, retains its original form. Wood paneling, commonly used before 1750, was the typical wall covering. In the room to the right of the entrance passage, paneling extends to the ceiling on the chimney wall, and halfway up the walls of both first-floor rooms. The Tarleton arms, it is said, once hung over the fireplace in the principal room. When the British officer Banastre Tarleton passed that way in 1780, he took the Tarleton coat of arms with him, but otherwise left the house untouched. To the major's restraint we owe the survival of Rock Castle and even of Monticello, for he could have burned either one.

The original site still may be clearly traced. It faced south to the river, and to the east of the site, on a direct axis with the house, are the remains of the old garden squares. (See fig. 69.) What could be more suggestive of Enniscorthy than this? Terraces, in this case, were laid out north of the garden, as there was not room before the cliff dropped away to the south. Nor had Emily Ann forgotten her English yew, probably brought from brother Tucker Coles's garden at Tallwood.

Surely Emily Ann, youngest of the Enniscorthy daughters, would have felt at home here. We see her in a pencil drawing (fig. 70) by William Henry Furness, Jr., as she must have looked at about the time that the new front was built. The longer one looks at the Rock Castle setting, the more old Enniscorthy comes to mind. The trees and the garden are the same; but the river, not the mountains, informs the view.

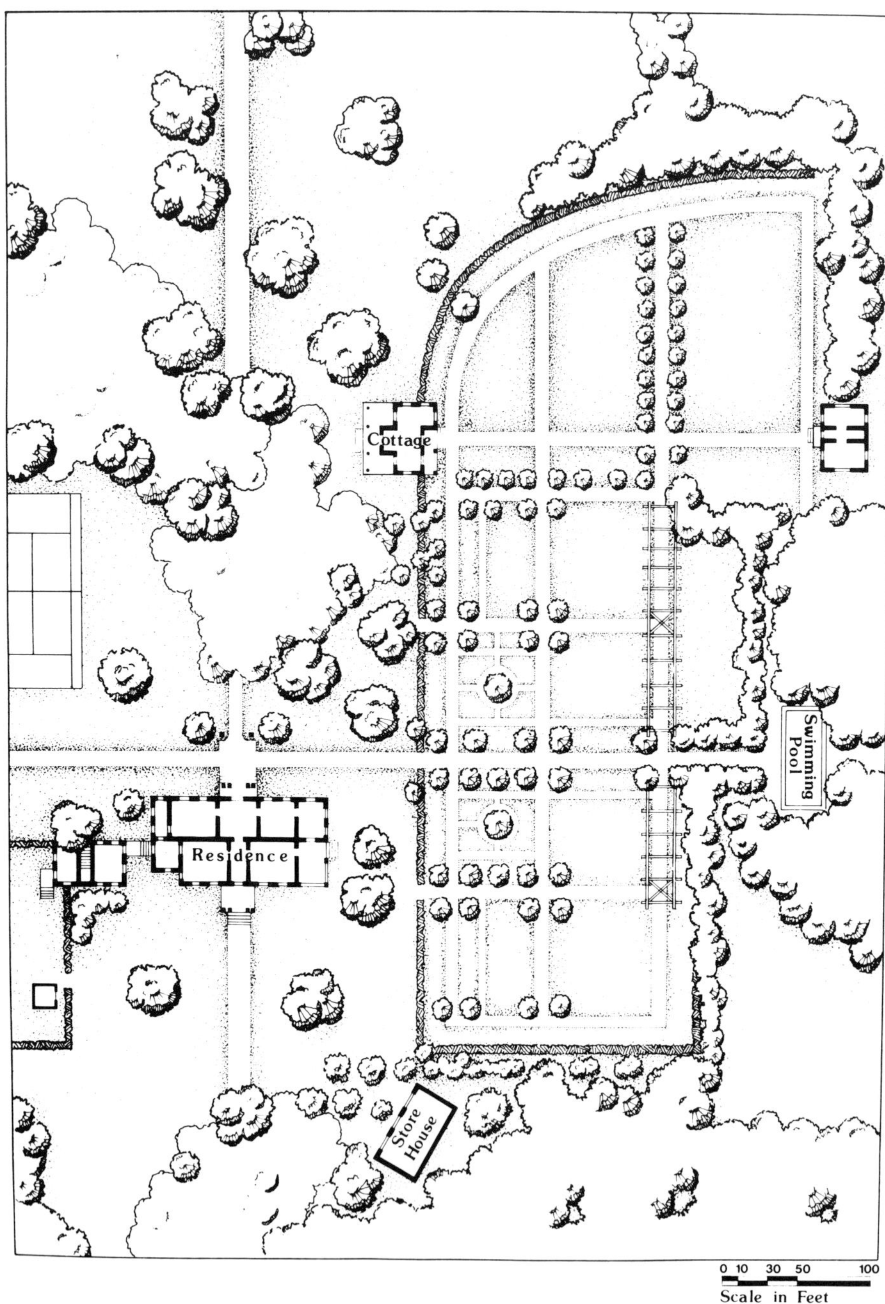

69.
Rock Castle, garden. In this 1923 site plan the house is shown on its original site, on a bluff overlooking the James and standing among great trees. The garden—laid out in rectilinear beds east of the house—includes English yews, possibly from Tallwood. (James River Garden Club, Historic Gardens of Virginia *[Richmond: William Byrd Press, 1923], opposite p. 28; redrawn by Patricia A. Fiedler, 1984, under the supervision of William D. Rieley.)*

70.
Emily Ann Coles Rutherfoord (Mrs. John Rutherfoord), 1795–1877, pencil drawing by William Henry Furness, Jr., c. 1840–50. (Property of Mrs. Helen Skinner; photo courtesy Mrs. William C. Cabell.)

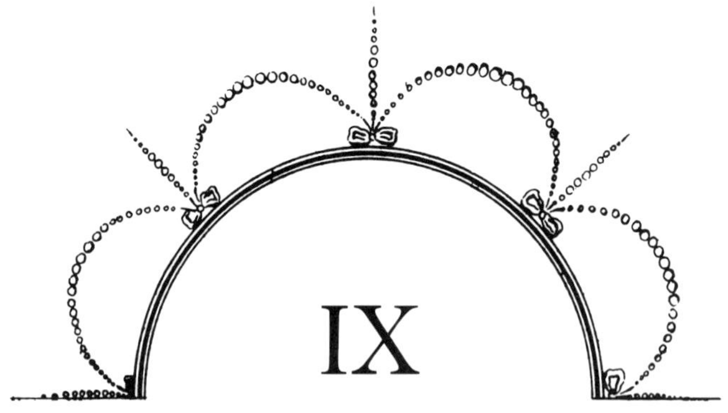

IX

Edward, 1786–1868

Land and Negroes in Virginia are to nine persons out of ten certain ruin, and to all certain expense, and uncertain profit, and trouble, and vexation of spirit, that wearies one of life.

Martha Jefferson Randolph to Nicholas Trist

Before we close this chronicle of a Virginia family, we must take a look at their attitude toward the "peculiar institution" to which their fate was inexorably linked. Martha Jefferson Randolph, Jefferson's daughter, had found it a fatal burden. Did the Coles find it so?

Walter at Woodville, Tucker at Tallwood, and even Miss Betsy showed concern for individual slaves. Miss Betsy's will, for example, provided a legacy to be paid monthly to Catherine Alexander, "a free woman of color,"[1] but Isaac's rather conventional letter to Cabell about slave uprisings (quoted in chapter VI) is the only evidence I have found of anything like the uneasiness expressed by Martha Randolph concerning the institution of slavery. Helen expressed the family attitude when she wrote from Philadelphia reassuring her sister that she need not fear the effect on any servant (they never used the word *slave*) of accompanying the family to Philadelphia, for the simple reason that "were it not for the galling word slavery,"[2] they were so much better off than the servant class in a northern city. True so far as it went; even Helen qualified her statement by referring to "good masters." It is hardly necessary to comment today on how limited was this view of freedom.

In the Enniscorthy family there was one striking exception. John II's youngest son, Edward, came home from The College of William and Mary in 1807 convinced that slavery was morally wrong. His father

71.
Rockfish River house of Edward Coles. The original log-pen section of this house was built by Thomas Meriwether, c. 1735. (Photo by K. Edward Lay, 1983.)

might well have feared the effect of education on this particular son. Edward interpreted the words "All men are created equal" to mean all men, black and white, nor did he hesitate to point out the contradictions that he saw around him. Bishop James Madison, the president of Edward's college, had to defend himself as best he might from the challenges of this confident young student. The bishop admitted that "slavery could not be justified in principle, and could only be tolerated . . . because of the difficulty of getting rid of it."[3]

Apparently, Edward had spoken out everywhere but at home. John II would hardly have set up this last son as a planter if he had known him to be determined to free his slaves the moment they were given to him. At his father's death in 1808 Edward in fact inherited 782 acres in Amherst (now Nelson) County, a beautiful mountain section some twenty miles southwest of the Coles land in Albemarle. Edward's farm, originally patented in 1735 by Thomas Meriwether, lay on both sides of the little Rockfish River. When John II bought it from Meriwether's son Francis in 1784, it contained a small log house—cited in the deed as "the house that you [Meriwether] live in"—and some modest outbuildings. In 1790 John II's account book shows that he paid a tax in Amherst County on seven Negroes and nine horses. In these years there was a white overseer on the Rockfish farm.

Edward, although the youngest son, could have expected a start in life not very different from his father's when he had came to Enniscorthy some forty years before. It is striking that the house on the Rockfish River no doubt resembled John I's original Enniscorthy. The single-pen log structure at Rockfish is still visible beneath the modern additions and new aluminum siding. (See figs. 71, 72a, b.) This Mer-

72.
Rockfish River house, measured drawings: (a) *first-floor plan—log-pen walls are heavily outlined in black;* (b) *section and elevation of house, showing log pen. (Drawings by Cathleen Ganzel, 1982, under the direction of K. Edward Lay.)*

A

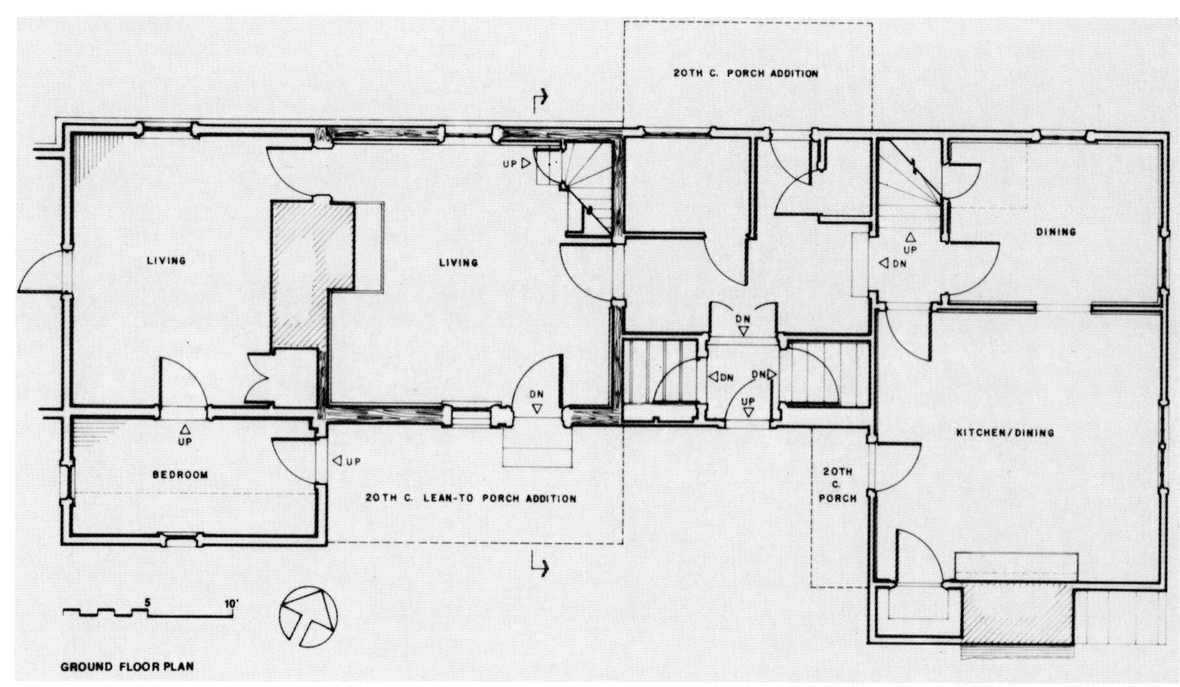

B

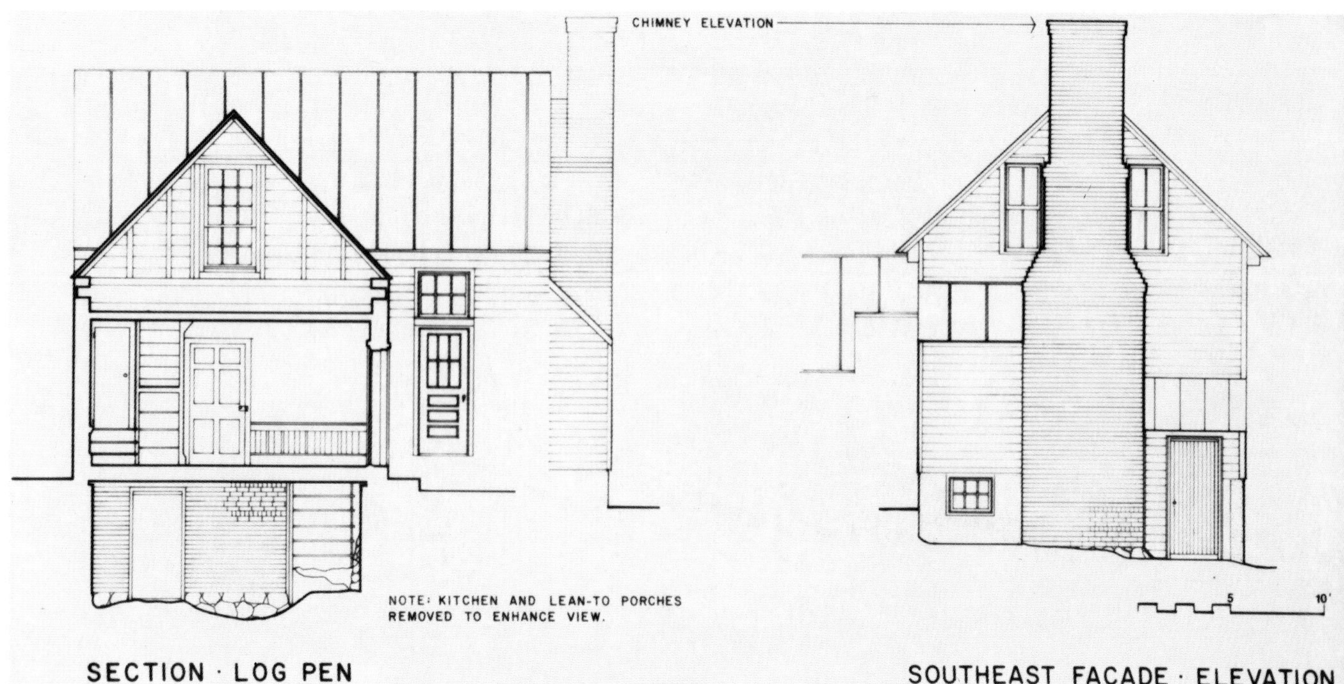

iwether house, like Enniscorthy, had stood on an isolated hilltop in the wilderness. It was built of V-notched logs and had a large brick gable and chimney, now partially concealed by additional inside walls. One of the old nine-over-six windows may still be seen at one end of this old section of the house. The deed that John Coles acquired in 1784 ends with the traditional words: "To have and to hold. . . . for himself and his heirs and assigns that he and they shall forever hereafter peaceably and quietly hold and enjoy."[4]

When John II had passed this land on to his son, he was no doubt confident that Edward too would peaceably and quietly hold and enjoy. Edward had no such intention, or certainly not in the way his father had in mind. Changes in the world around him, and above all in his own moral attitude, made Edward's story a quite different one. He was haunted, as other members of his family were not, by the moral dilemma. When the Rockfish farm and twenty slaves became his, he declared his intention to his family: he would free his slaves. In Edward's later account of this family crisis he relates that his brothers attempted to reason him out of such an extraordinary act. They said that a planter without slaves is like a carpenter without tools. They asked, How did he expect to live? They pointed, inexorably, to the law, passed two years before, that no freed slave could remain in the state for more than one year after attaining his freedom.[5]

The recent slave uprising of 1800 in Haiti had struck fear into the hearts of the plantation society. In that same year Gabriel's Rebellion, abortive as it was, had carried the danger, the threat of whites massacred by blacks, into Virginia itself. Edward's plan at first had been simply to free his slaves without registering their freedom papers. It soon became evident that his neighbors, not to speak of his family, could not tolerate such an incendiary example. Edward's ideas were dynamite. Perhaps at twenty-two the young man himself hardly recognized their potential for blowing up a whole society. The pressure upon him was immense; beseiged by family and by such influential family friends as Madison and Monroe, he finally agreed to go to Washington as private secretary to President Madison, to gain, as they urged him, more knowledge of the world before taking an irrevocable step.

In taking this position he was simply following his brother Isaac, who had served Jefferson in the same capacity. While enjoying some five years in the household of his cousins James and Dolley Madison, Edward never for a moment lost sight of his resolve concerning his slaves. On the mountain farm that he had left behind in Virginia, he made the slave Ralph Crawford his overseer. Absentee ownership worked no better for Edward than it did for Thomas Jefferson; in 1812 he complained in a letter from Washington that Rockfish "has not been able to pay off $500 in four years."[6]

Before the end of his time with the Madisons, the president had sent him on a diplomatic mission to Russia, which Edward completed with a grand tour of Europe. It was this sophisticated young man who set out to explore the wild western country; the end in view, of course, was to discover a land where slaves might live successfully in freedom, but much intervened before the final step was taken.

During two summers, of 1815 and 1818, Edward explored the land beyond the settlements, in Ohio, Indiana, and Illinois. The area chosen was the prairie land of Illinois, east of a bend of the Mississippi near the town of Edwardsville. It was not until the spring of 1819 that Edward at last made the long-intended move. He gathered his people together and sent them on the first leg of their journey in charge of his headman, the black Ralph Crawford. They were to meet at Brownsville, Pennsylvania. Edward, traveling on horseback, passed the little party, he went on to buy the necessary keelboats for the voyage down the Ohio. At this point he was not able to forego a letter of mild triumph to his skeptical brother John in Virginia. "I have particular pleasure in telling you that however correct you may be in general, you are not infallible in your prophesies. Your predictions as to my man Ralph and his party have proved erroneous at least so far, so that I passed them just beyond Laurel Hill, about thirty miles from this (place). . . . all safe and getting on remarkably well." It was part of his great experiment, to show that Ralph Crawford had "conducted the party with as much judgement and economy as anyone, even of the glorious Saxon race, could have done."[7]

At the request of his family, Edward had not revealed his plans for their freedom to Ralph and his people before leaving Virginia. It was on the Ohio that the great moment came. As the keel boats drifted lazily down the river Edward called his people together. It was a beautiful April morning. The announcement, Edward felt, should be made in as nearly one sentence as possible. "Free," he said. "You are no longer slaves, but free." (See fig. 73.) For a long moment there was no sound. Then a sort of hysterical giggling laugh began, passing from one to another. The people looked at Edward, and they looked at each other. Still no one spoke.[8]

They were free, Edward told them, free as he was: free to stay with him or to go ashore at their pleasure. There were cries of "Oh, no. Oh, no!" Ralph Crawford stepped forward. He said that none of them ought to go free until they had paid for their passage. They should help

73.
This mural in the capitol building at Springfield, Illinois, represents Edward Coles on the Ohio River at the moment of freeing his slaves. (Photo courtesy Illinois State Historical Library, Springfield.)

Edward get settled on his new Illinois farm. The others agreed, demanding, How will you live if you set us free?[9] They put the question with even greater conviction than had Edward's own family. This is an attitude often overlooked: the pride that many slaves felt in the dependence of their masters.

Edward's land was three quarters in prairie and the rest in timber; a few acres were enclosed, where there was a deserted log cabin. So Edward started again, this time with free, not slave, labor, on what he called his Prairie Land Farm. The untamed prairie grass stood breast high, waving in the wind, "the land so tough and hard," he wrote Madison, "that it required my whole team to pull one plough."[10]

This new Westerner, however, was no Abe Lincoln, nor did he work the tough land himself. He lived in Edwardsville, where he attended to his business as registrar of lands in the new state, visiting the farm each afternoon. Once again the blacks were in charge. The system of dependency was ingrained, and it worked both ways. Edward's account books, now in the Illinois State Historical Library show that in the years 1819–32 he continued to care for his people: "For wine for Ralph when sick," was an early item.[11] Many such items occur in the accounts, in addition to payment for work performed.

One expense was essential to the conclusion of his experiment. On that great freedom day on the river he had promised each head of family, or male over the age of twenty-three, a quarter section (160 acres) of land. It was this that had brought a glow to Ralph Crawford's usually impassive face. "They seldom speak of their freedom," Edward noted, "without speaking, and that too rather in a consequential way, of their lands."[12] It was what made freedom real. It also left Edward, along with a bond he was forced to put up lest the freed slaves should become wards of the state, pretty strapped financially.

Ralph Crawford did not live long to enjoy his freedom, but his brother Robert did. Coles's deed to Robert Crawford reflects the full, almost mystic powers conveyed by land: "To have and to hold the above granted, bargained and described with the appurtenances, unto the said Robert Crawford, his heirs and assigns forever."[13] Robert went on to become a preacher and founding member of the Black Methodist Church of Illinois. Edward never lost touch with these people. Years later, after he himself had removed to Philadelphia, he received a letter from "Preacher" Crawford: "We was truly thankful that our old master John Cowles and his wife Rebeckah ever had a son born by the name of Edward," words that must have brought a glow to Edward's heart.[14]

His years in Illinois were filled with political battles in the antislavery cause. The proslavery party wished to hold a convention in order to declare Illinois a slave state. Edward led the opposition, and in the close election of 1822 he was elected governor of the state. It had been a near thing, but Illinois remained free. This was to have a critical effect on the war to come.

After two troubled terms as governor, Edward was defeated in a bid for Congress from the divided state. After all, he was not a man of the frontier. He was anti-Jackson in a time and place when Jackson was sweeping all before him, but he could be sure now that the Crawfords and their fellows were well established in a free state. It was after this defeat that Edward retired, perhaps thankfully, to Philadelphia. In Virginia, by his one great act, the freeing of his slaves, he had closed all political doors behind him. In Philadelphia, where almost no one owned slaves, he found the life most suited to his taste.

His portrait by Henry Inman (fig. 74) done in Philadelphia in 1832

74.
Governor Edward Coles, 1786–1868, oil on canvas by Henry Inman, 1832. (Photo by Gitchell Studio, Charlottesville, Va.)

75.
Capt. Roberts Coles, 1838–62. (Copy of a photograph taken by Vanderoth, Taylor, and Brown, Philadelphia, c. 1860, courtesy Oliver Robbins.)

shows the vigorous man still at the height of his powers. He married the daughter of a wealthy Quaker family; he had three children; he attended the famous Wistar parties, an informal discussion group that represented the social and intellectual summit in that Quaker city; but no public position was ever offered him. There were distressful moments when Virginia relatives passed through the city without stopping to see him; there were happy times when he and his family, now including two boys and a girl, visited the Madisons and his brothers in Virginia. Above all, now there was his joy in his son Roberts.

This second son was named after his mother's Philadelphia family, but it was Roberts (fig. 75), not his elder brother, Edward, who resembled the Coles. Roberts was far more gay and sprightly than the other two children. He was devoted to his father. It was Roberts who had inherited the exiled father's passionate love of Virginia. As soon as he reached his majority, Roberts went back. He bought land, largely on credit, from his cousin Tucker Coles. It was called the Plantation Tract, and lay just north of his Uncle John's property. All had once been a part of old Enniscorthy.

No prodigal son could have returned with more joy than did this young man, an exile through no wish of his own. However the fatality of such a step was already ordained. "I claim my share of paternity in Enniscorthy," he wrote a friend. "When Virginia was invaded and its existence threatened, I volunteered."[15] He fought not for slavery, not for anything specific perhaps, but just for the homeland. Roberts's last words, in the letter he wrote to his fiancée as the Confederate troops prepared to storm Roanoke Island, were "Now I strike for Virginia."[16] And striking thus for Virginia, he died. Captain Roberts Coles was killed in 1862, in the battle of Roanoke Island.

For Edward his son's choice was as bitter as death. To his brother-in-law John Rutherfoord he wrote: "There is little or no prospect of my ever again being happy."[17] Three years later the cause to which Edward had devoted his own life was won: the slaves were free. The South lay prostrate, the cost fully paid. For Edward it had been the blood of his son.

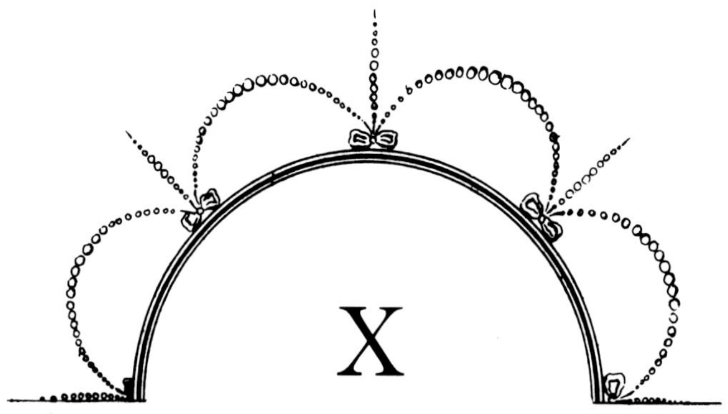

X

Enniscorthy III

A gale was blowing from the north west. . . .

In the last week of 1839 Enniscorthy stood on that long-established site on the Green Mountain; widely scattered family and friends called it home. For the Coles it was Enniscorthy—its fields, its mills, its slave cabins, and its great rambling house—that had set the pattern, and sheltered the life-style that we have sketched in these pages. In 1839 one did not doubt that it would last forever.

Isaac, stepping out over his well-tended lawn beneath carefully landscaped trees, had gone into a Charlottesville Court Day and been elected to the state legislature in Richmond. Julianna, who suffered from what Helen called the "Swiss disease," that is to say homesickness, was at home again after visiting friends in Baltimore. She had been to the theater. The heir, John Stricker, and the bright little sister, Isaetta, were playing indoors on that wintry day, the last Monday of December 1839. A gale was blowing from the north west. From some hearth or chimney a shower of sparks had risen; flames had caught and gone roaring with the wind against the gable end of the house. Once started, no effort availed, the whole house went. Only the portraits and some furniture were saved.[1]

Isaac and Julianna had urgent invitations to take refuge with any number of relatives, but preferred to make do on their own property, probably in whatever remained of John I's first house on the land, which could have accounted for the remodeling later see in the Cabin in the Grove. All seemed to be going fairly well. Isaac was serving as planned in the state legislature, and had been reelected for the session of 1841, when suddenly, and apparently quite unexpectedly, he died.

Left behind were Julianna and the two small children, John Stricker, born 1832, and Julia Isaetta, born 1831.

Knowing Isaac, we can easily believe that he had set to work to design a new house on the old site at the time of his death. There is evidence, which we cannot at this time authenticate, that this indeed had been the case, but if so, another nine years were to pass before his widow raised a new Enniscorthy on the foundations of the old.

As we know, it was not the first time that a Coles widow had been left with young children and a large estate. Mary Ann Winston, John I's widow, had married again; whether she had taken an interest in the plantations left her children we do not know, but those eighteenth-century tobacco plantations had surely been maintained as going and profitable concerns until the children were ready to take over their inheritance. The 1840s presented a somewhat different picture. Albemarle planters were among the most scientific farmers in the state: they were well aware of soil erosion, and many, like Thomas Mann Randolph, Jefferson's son-in-law, had adopted ploughing on the contour to avoid erosion of the precious soil. Tucker Coles, in particular, was active in the highly thought of Albemarle Agricultural Society.

It was not enough. They were substituting wheat for tobacco and planting clover to restore the exhausted fields, but the price system (low for exports, high for imports) was against them, and so was the declining fertility of the soil, which could no longer support the increasing population of slaves. The only way to stay solvent in Virginia was to sell slaves down the river, as the saying goes, to work the cotton and sugar plantations of the deep south. This was a course that decent masters, such as the Coles, the Madisons, the Jeffersons, refused to take. It violated the real sense of responsibility that they felt for their "people." The plight of a man as prudent and honorable as ex-President Madison is well illustrated by his letter of October 3, 1834, to his friend Edward Coles. Madison was in financial difficulties: "Finding that I have, in order to avoid the sale of Negroes sold land until the residue will not support them, concentered and increasing as they are, I have yielded to the necessity of parting with some of them to a friend and kinsman [W. Taylor], who I am persuaded will do better by them than I can, and to whom they gladly consent to be transferred. By this transaction I am enabled to replace the sum you kindly loaned me."[2]

Clearly the position of Julianna Stricker Coles, Isaac's widow, differed substantially in 1841 from that of John I's widow in 1747, or even from the position of those other formidable ladies Jean Skipwith, widowed in 1804, and Eliza Coles Carter, in 1809. Juliana was a city girl, born and bred in Baltimore. Isaac had died in May 1841. Less than a year later, in January of 1842, she had bought two adjoining lots in Charlottesville at what is now 303 East High Street,[3] and by 1845 she had completed building a handsome double-pile brick house (fig. 76a), valued at $2,250 in the tax lists of that year. The design of this house, built some five years before she set to work to rebuild Enniscorthy for the son and heir, John Stricker, shows that Julianna was up to the latest styles in architecture, at least when building for herself. The High Street house shows more sophisticated detail than Enniscorthy III, which was finally built in 1850. Italianate brackets support the porch roof in Charlottesville; there were full entablatures above the windows. The Greek Revival structure had a rectangular transom and sidelights at the door.

Only one Enniscorthy daughter had, in the thirties, no home of her own. She had hardly needed one. This was Miss Betsy, unmarried, and invited by her brother Isaac to keep house for him at Enniscorthy after their mother's death. Nor need we for one moment feel sorry for this independent single woman. Let Miss Betsy speak for herself: "I will never by any act of my own place myself in a state of perfect dependence. I shall always have to depend on my relations for kindness and protection, but I trust never for bread, meat and clothes."[4] Her father had left her a thousand pounds and seventy-two Negroes, and with this Miss Betsy made do for the rest of her life. Those Negroes that she did not need for personal service were hired out, to her brother or to others, a system often used by landless ladies to produce an income.

She was always a welcome visitor, and we may note that she usually visited wherever the gayest social life prevailed, such as Washington when her brother-in-law Stevenson was Jackson's Speaker. "Old Mr. King would certainly have made a Belle of me," she wrote to John III, "if Nature had given me the least pretension to the character."[5] Clearly the desire was not there either, for it may have appeared to Betsy that the career of a belle was short-lived, while that of single woman of independent means could, and did, last a lifetime. The downtrodden spinster aunt was not a figure common in Southern society. Betsy, of course, was fortunate in not desiring a career of greater scope than the one offered her by that society. She might, indeed, be considered one of its most typical members.

Now, after the loss of old Enniscorthy, she had no intention of becoming a perennial visitor. She soon followed her sister-in-law's example by buying a Charlottesville lot for herself, a purchase recorded in 1844. On this lot, later 522 Park Street, Miss Betsy built herself a Victorian single-pile brick house (fig. 76b). A shallow pediment above the center roofline and Italianate brackets supporting the veranda roof

76.
Coles houses in Charlottesville. (a) *303 East High Street house, c. 1845, home of Julianna Stricker Coles; 1913 photo. (Courtesy Mrs. V. H. Valentine.)* (b) *522 Park Street house, c. 1846, home of Elizabeth (Miss Betsy) Coles. The porch and the left wing are later additions. Note the Victorian detail; 1925 photo. (Courtesy Mrs. William Massie Smith.) Neither of these houses is standing today.*

A

B

77.
Enniscorthy III, built by Julianna Stricker Coles for her son, John Stricker Coles, in 1850. This early photo, taken in the 1920s, shows the original five-bay house with portico. The Greek Revival wings were added later in the 1850s. (Photo courtesy Elizabeth Langhorne.)

gave it style. This house was occupied by Sheridan's staff in 1865.[6] Miss Betsy retired, an old lady of seventy-four, to the Rutherfoords in Richmond, where the Yankees were all too soon to follow. Tradition has it that Miss Betsy died of fright in the siege of Richmond, but we prefer to think of her departing of her own accord with the advent of a new era, so definitely not her own.

Julianna, of course, was duty bound to build a house for her son before he came of age in 1853. Evidence on the site shows that she built on the central portion of the old foundations. Enniscorthy III (figs. 77, 78a, b, and 79) thus began as a single-pile brick house three bays wide. There was an eight-column veranda across the front. The front doorway is Greek Revival with no fanlight—as in the High Street house.

Some of the trees still standing at Enniscorthy date from this period, or from not too long thereafter, as do the pair of fine old holly trees that stand at the back of the 1850 house. They are appropriately named John and Rebecca. A hemlock and the great white oaks at the edge of the hollow survive today from the original forest.

John Stricker did not live long, if ever, in the new house at Enniscor-

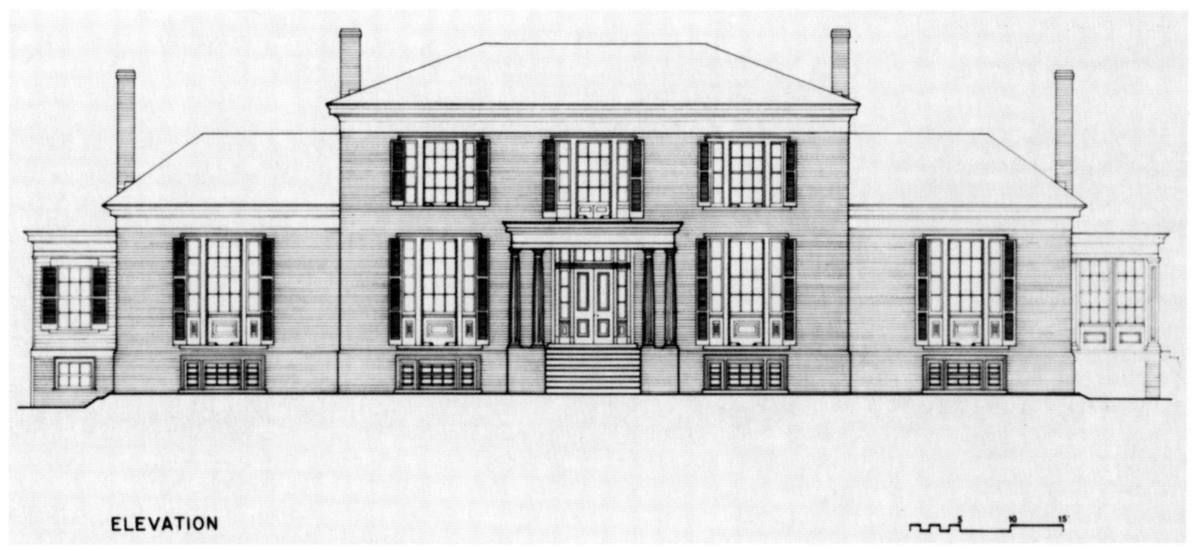

A

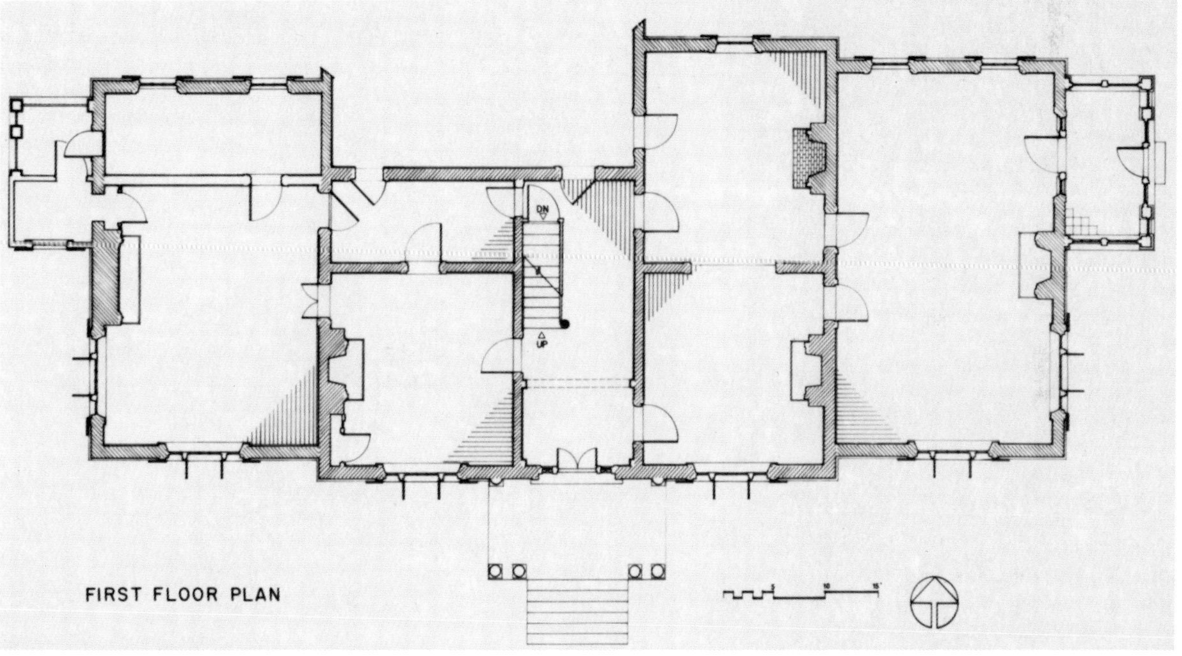

B

78.
Enniscorthy III, measured drawings: (a) *south elevation;* (b) *first-floor plan. (Drawings by Cathleen Ganzel, 1982, under the direction of K. Edward Lay.)*

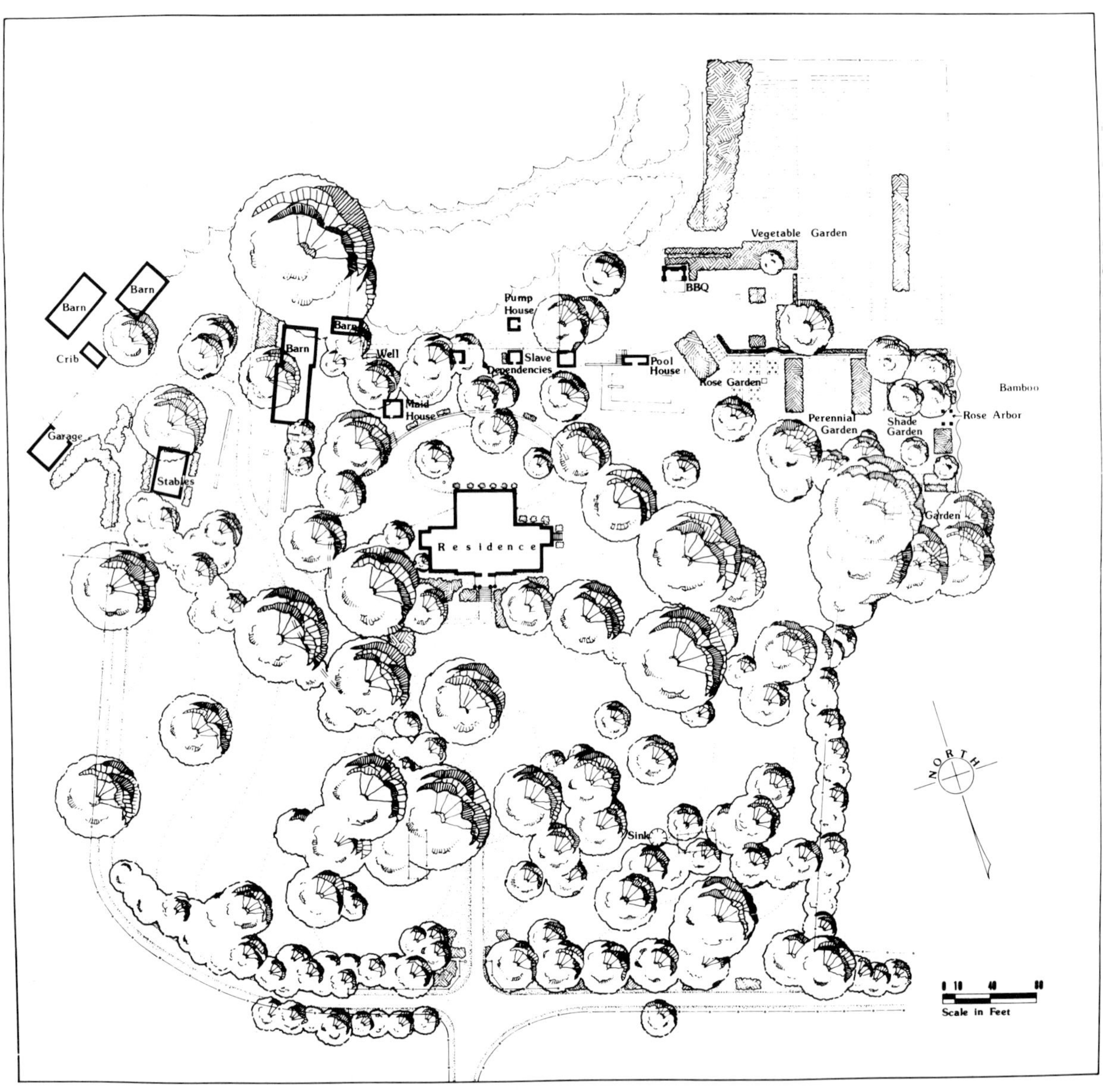

Vegetable Garden
Barn
Barn
BBQ
Pump House
Barn
Barn
Crib
Well
Slave Dependencies
Pool House
Rose Garden
Bamboo
Maid House
Perennial Garden
Shade Garden
Rose Arbor
Garage
Stables
Garden
Residence
NORTH
Sink
Scale in Feet

79.
Enniscorthy III, site plan. The gardens show elaboration by subsequent owners, extending the old garden site east of the house. Three still-existing eighteenth-century outbuildings are shown on a plantation street north of the house. Until recent years, a two-room cabin, similar to one at Estouteville (see fig. 55), existed at the east end of this street. (Drawing by Patricia A. Fiedler; based on research by Cynthia Fink, Bryan Katen, and Foster Paulette; under the supervision of William D. Rieley.)

thy, for in 1853 he married the daughter of Governor Pickens of South Carolina and removed to that state. In 1855 he sold Enniscorthy to his cousin Tucker Skipwith Coles, third son of the Estouteville family. Tucker added the two wings that balance the center section of the present Enniscorthy and also enlarged the house to the back, so that the north wall now rests on the old brick-pile foundation of John II's piazza. The rooms on this north side are somewhat irregular, so that the chronology of the various additions is a bit hard to trace. This much-remodeled house remained in the family until the death of Tucker's granddaughter, Lelia Coles Bennett, in 1925.

By the 1850s the center of gravity, certainly as represented by the family houses, had shifted from Enniscorthy to Estouteville. John III had died in 1848. Subject to his mother's life interest, the second son, Peyton Skipwith Coles, inherited the Estouteville house and land. Peyton's marriage to his first cousin, Julia Isaetta of Enniscorthy, took place in 1852 from her mother's house in Charlottesville, but the great week-long celebrations after the wedding were held at Estouteville. We see both of these young people (figs. 80, 81) and Selina herself (see fig. 36) in the portraits that she had painted by L. M. D. Guillaume. The Rives family of Castle Hill had encouraged this young artist to come over from Paris. He had come to Albemarle specifically to paint a Rives horse, but found many human subjects eager to sit for their likenesses in the new realistic style. It may have been at this time too that the walls of the great hall were newly decorated. Here Peyton and the greatly beloved "Miss Isa" were to live and raise eleven of the ten sons and two daughters born to them. At Isaetta's death in 1907 Estouteville was put on the market, and it was sold in 1910.

Old Woodville went out of the family in 1886. Some time after the death of Walter Coles, Jr., Walter, Sr., had given his younger son Edward six hundred acres on Biscuit Run about five miles south of Charlottesville, where in 1854 he built a brick house, Richland (fig. 82), in the Greek Revival style. Here Edward Coles lived until his death in 1883. The land was then divided among his children, and shortly thereafter the house itself was sold. In 1858 Walter's second son, Isaac Tucker Coles, purchased some 600 acres south of the Tallwood tract, which remained in this branch of the family until the close of 1899.[7]

By 1865 Tucker and Helen had both departed. Tucker, the most public-spirited of the family, had left a considerable sum for the promotion of public education in the county. The Tallwood estate went to Peyton Skipwith Coles, Jr., when he should attain his majority. Hard times were closing in on the Coles as on all Southern families, and Peyton sold Tallwood in 1898. Their world was coming to an end,

80.
Peyton Skipwith Coles, 1826–87, oil on wood panel by L. M. D. Guillaume, 1857. (Photo courtesy Mrs. James Umstattd.)

81.
Julia Isaetta Coles (Mrs. Peyton Skipwith Coles), 1831–1907, oil on wood panel by L. M. D. Guillaume, 1857. (Photo courtesy Mrs. James Umstattd.)

82.
Richland, built 1854 by Walter Coles for his son Edward. (Photo by K. Edward Lay.)

not with a bang, but surely not with a whimper. When no native Southerner had any money anyway, the Coles continued to congregate at Tallwood and Estouteville. Especially at bachelor-inhabited Tallwood, the young people had a very good time. Miss Isa managed somehow to give her boys an education, but the farm no longer offered a livelihood. They ventured forth to such alien soil as Nebraska, Philadelphia, and even New York. Redlands alone has never been sold. "Miss Sally" and "Miss Polly" Carter are remembered as the founders of St. Timothy's School in Catonsville, Maryland; and it is due to their success that Redlands remains in family hands today.

Epilogue

After 1865, when people could in some measure pick themselves up and try to live again, Tucker Coles repossessed the farm that Captain Roberts Coles had bought after the return of the unpaid mortgage and $5,000 from Roberts's father. Tucker started to build there, where Roberts had planned a house. Two unfinished columns stand on a low ridge, but no house was ever raised. The age of the plantations had come to an end; of that past era only the buildings, and perhaps a lingering tradition, remain.

Redlands stands among its great trees and Estouteville on its green mountain, both virtually unchanged. Additions to Old Woodville and the present Enniscorthy have not essentially changed their character. Only the Charlottesville houses have disappeared, replaced by later development. With the exception of Tallwood, all the surviving houses are lived in today. If the plantation house is a work of art, then these houses are timeless symbols, reflecting a departed life.

Fine detail, a sense of classical space and order—were these things mere pretensions, or were they an essential part of the Virginian self-image? Appearances may go to the very heart of character. Isaac Coles never shook the world with his accomplishments, but we think of him, and of men like him, when we stand in his house. It is, not one family alone, but a whole vanished culture that these houses represent.

In our study we have portrayed the life, and above all the changes in building and taste that four generations produced. It was, in fact, a sort of odyssey, a journey from log pen to brick mansion, that we may follow in this dual history of a family and of the houses that they built.

83.
Plan of Coles family graveyard, Enniscorthy, Keene, Va. (Drawn by Foster Paulette under the supervision of William D. Rieley.)

GATE

George Minor Coles	Roberts Coles			
	Mary Minor Coles	Anne Elizabeth Brown		Tucker Skipwith Coles
				Unnamed son of Tucker S. Coles
		Elizabeth Franklin		Unnamed dau. of Tucker S. Coles
				S.
				Peyton Skipwith
				Marion Deveaux Singleton
		Peyton Skipwith Coles	Arthur N. Coles	
		Mary Norris Coles	William Bedford Coles	Peyton Skipwith Coles
	Bertha Stricker Coles	Henry Aylett Coles	Edmund Lyons MacKenzie	Julia Isaetta Coles
(Walter Lippincott Coles)	Bertha Lippincott Coles	Kenneth Roderick MacKenzie	Julia Stricker MacKenzie	Selina Skipwith Coles
(Frances Sadtler Coles)	Stricker Coles	Isaac Coles	Grace Stuart MacKenzie	Travis Tucker Coles

		John Bowler Coles	Ellen Monroe Carter		
John Skipwith Coles	Roberts Coles (Removed)		Sally Logan Coles		
John Coles	Helen Coles	Sally T. Coles	Elizabeth Cocke Coles		
Selina Coles	Tucker Coles	Walter Coles	Walter Coles		
Selina Skipwith Coles	Elizabeth Coles	Eliza F. Cocke Coles	Anne Elizabeth Carter Coles		
	Rebecca Elizabeth Coles		James Carter Coles		
Andrew Stevenson	John Coles	James Currie, Jr.		Elizabeth Noland Carter	
Sarah Coles Stevenson	John Coles		Margaret Smith Carter	Robert S. Carter	
Frances Arnett Stevenson	Isaac Coles	Rebecca E. Tucker	Robert Hill Carter		Unnamed sons (2) of Robert & Bessie Carter
Edward Coles	William Coles		Caryanne Smith Carter	Alice Blair Carter	
John E. Coles	Thomas Rutherford		Louise Carter	Robert Hill Carter	
Peyton Skipwith Coles	Rebecca Elizabeth Rutherford	Edward Champe Carter			
Isaac A. Coles	Helen Coles Rutherford	Robert Carter			
Julia Coles		Mary Eliza Carter			
		Rebecca Isaetta Carter	Mary Eliza Rives		

Notes

INTRODUCTION

1. Heather A. Clemenson, *English Country Houses and Landed Estates* (New York: St. Martin's Press, 1982).

I

1. William Byrd II, *Another Secret Diary*, ed. Maude Woodfin (Richmond: Dietz Press, 1942).
2. William Bedford Coles, *The Coles Family of Virginia* (New York: privately printed, 1931), p. 37.
3. *Richmond Times Dispatch*, Sept. 8, 1937, p. 7.
4. Coles, *The Coles Family*, p. 38. *Journal of the Council of Virginia* quoted from *Virginia Magazine of History and Biography* 15 (1907–8): 114.
5. Brunswick County Deed Books 3 and 1, Virginia State Library, Richmond, Va.
6. Robert Carter to Colonel John Tayloe, Jan. 29, 1729, Smith-Carter Papers (acc. no. 1729), Manuscripts Department, University of Virginia Library, Charlottesville, Va.
7. Rev. Edgar Woods, *History of Albemarle County in Virginia* (Bridgewater, Va.: The Greek Bookman, 1932), p. 2.
8. *The Secret Diary of William Byrd*, ed. Louis B. Wright and Marion Tinling (Richmond, Dietz Press, 1941), p. 267.
9. Jay Worrall, Jr., "The Albemarle Quakers," *Magazine of Albemarle County History* 40 (1982): 25–44.
10. Quoted in Coles, *The Coles Family*, p. 42.
11. Ibid.
12. Quoted in Virginius Dabney, *Richmond, the Story of a City* (New York: Doubleday, 1976), p. 12.
13. Byrd quoted in *Richmond Times Dispatch*, Sept. 8, 1937, p. 7.
14. Louis H. Manarin, *The History of Henrico County* (Charlottesville: University Press of Virginia, 1984), p. 99.
15. Coles, *The Coles Family*, p. 42.
16. "The Vestry Book of Henrico Parish, Virginia, 1730–1773," in Dr. R. A. Brock, *Annals of Henrico Parish, Addendum* (Richmond: The Trustees of St. John's Church, 1904), p. 73.
17. Quoted in Coles, *The Coles Family*, p. 42.
18. J. F. D. Smyth, *Tour in the United States of America* (1784), quoted in Mary Wingfield Scott, *Houses of Old Richmond* (New York: Bonanza Books, 1941), p. 12.
19. Scott, *Houses of Old Richmond*, p. 12.
20. Dabney, *Richmond*, p. 22.

II

1. Nathaniel Mason Paulette, *Historic Roads of Virginia: Albemarle County Roads, 1725–1816* (Charlottesville: Virginia Highway and Transportation Research Council, 1981), p. 56.
2. J. Hector St. John de Crevecoeur, *Letters from an American Farmer* (London: Dent, 1912).
3. Carl Bridenbaugh. *Myths and Realities: Societies of the Colonial South* (1952; reprint, New York: Atheneum, 1963), p. 156.
4. Count Castiglioni, quoted in A. J. Morrison, ed., *Travels in Virginia in Revolutionary Times* (Lynchburg, Va.: J. P. Bell Co., 1922), p. 67.
5. Isaac Coles of Halifax County served in the First Continental Congress and married the fashionable Catherine Thompson of New York.
6. William Bedford Coles, *The Coles Family of Virginia* (New York: privately printed, 1931), opposite p. 18.
7. Rebecca Elizabeth Coles to Rebecca Elizabeth Tucker, Aug. 8, 1773 (M2C6786b), Virginia Historical Society, Richmond.
8. John Coles to Rebecca Elizabeth Coles, Aug. 26, 30, 1775, Smith-Carter Papers (acc. no. 1729), Manuscripts Department, University of Virginia Library.
9. Thomas Jefferson's 1767 Memorandum Book, miscellaneous section, c. July 5, 1769, Thomas Jefferson Papers, Department of Manuscripts, University of Virginia Library.
10. John Coles Account Book, July 1774, p. 53 (acc. no. 9533), Manuscripts Department, University of Virginia Library.
11. Hening's *Statutes* (Richmond, 1821), 8:93.
12. We may note that the name of this builder was spelt in various ways: Weathered, Wetherhead, and Wethered. The first name could be given as Francis or Frank.
13. John Coles Account Book, July 1774, p. 52, University of Virginia Library.
14. Irving Papers, quoted courtesy of Mrs. Bernard Rosenberger.
15. John Coles Account Book, 1799, p. 223, University of Virginia Library.
16. John Hammond Moore, *Albemarle: Jefferson's County, 1727–1976* (Charlottesville: University Press of Virginia, 1976), p. 81.
17. Mrs. Drummond to Thomas Jefferson, Williamsburg, Mar. 12, 1771, in *Papers of Thomas Jefferson*, ed. Julian Boyd, vol. 1 (Princeton, N.J.: Princeton University Press, 1950), p. 65.

18. *Virginia, a Guide to the Old Dominion* (New York: Oxford University Press, 1956), p. 636.
19. Thomas Jefferson's Account Book, Jan. 20, 1774, p. 169, Thomas Jefferson Papers, Department of Manuscripts, University of Virginia Library.
20. Betsy Coles to Capt. John Coles, Georgetown, Jan. 17, 1824, private collection.
21. Andrew Drummond to John Coles, Apr. 5, 1780, Smith-Carter Papers (acc. no. 1729), Manuscripts Department, University of Virginia Library.
22. Coles, *The Coles Family*, pp. 18, 19.
23. George Maclaren Brydon, *Virginia's Mother Church* (Philadelphia: Church Historical Society, 1952), 2:362–63.
24. John Coles Account Book, 1783, p. 81, University of Virginia Library.
25. Conversation with Joseph Agee, formerly employed at Enniscorthy and descendant of Coles slaves.
26. Mrs. Harrison Smith, *The First Forty Years of Washington Society* (New York: Frederick Ungar, 1965), p. 68.
27. John Coles Account Book, 1783, p. 101, University of Virginia Library.
28. Philip Miller, *The Gardener's Kalendar*, 14th ed. (London, 1765), p. 229.
29. Martha Jefferson Randolph to Thomas Jefferson, Jan. 16, 1791, in *The Family Letters of Thomas Jefferson*, ed. Edwin Betts and James A. Bear (Columbia: University of Missouri Press, 1966), p. 68.
30. John Coles Account Book, 1795, p. 211, University of Virginia Library.
31. Hannah Glasse, *The Art of Cookery Made Plain and Easy* (London: printed for A. Millar, J. R. Tonson, etc., 1765). (Courtesy of Mrs. Gordon Roberts.)
32. John Coles Account Book, 1784, p. 119, University of Virginia Library.
33. Ibid., 1785, p. 122.
34. Fiske Kimball, *Domestic Architecture of the American Colonies and of the Early Republic* (New York: Dover, 1966), p. 99.
35. John Coles Account Book, 1786, p. 119, University of Virginia Library.
36. "Memoirs of a Monticello Slave," *Jefferson at Monticello*, ed. James A. Bear, Jr. (Charlottesville: University Press of Virginia, 1967), p. 20.
37. Mutual Assurance Society Records, no. 351, vol. 13, reel 2 (1799), and no. 2274, vol. 45, reel 5 (1810), Virginia Historic Landmarks Commission, Richmond.
38. Dr. Charles Everette to Rebecca Coles, Feb. 15, 1815, Smith-Carter Papers (acc. no. 1729), Manuscripts Department, University of Virginia Library.
39. John Coles Account Book, 1785–86, p. 140, University of Virginia Library.
40. Coles, *The Coles Family Book*, p. 56.
41. John Coles to Isaac Coles, Dec. 26, 1796, private collection.

III

1. Isaac A. Coles to Joseph C. Cabell, Washington, July 6, 1807, private collection.
2. Isaac A. Coles to Joseph C. Cabell, Washington, July 17, 1807, private collection.
3. Fillmore Norfleet, *Saint Mémin in Virginia: Portraits and Biographies* (Richmond, Va.: Dietz Press, 1942), pp. 13, 14.
4. Ibid., p. 25.
5. Thomas Jefferson to James Madison, Apr. 11, 1818, quoted in Bradford L. Rauschenberg, "William John Coffee, Sculptor-Painter," *Journal of Early Southern Decorative Arts*, Nov. 1978, p. 31.
6. Ibid., pp. 30, 31.

IV

1. Will of Walter Coles, 1854, Albemarle County Will Book 23, p. 37, County Clerk's Office, Charlottesville, Va.
2. Edgemont is believed to have been designed by Jefferson for James Powell Cocke. It stands on what is now the Keene–North Garden Road. For Church Road and Fry's path see William Bedford Coles, *The Coles Family of Virginia* (New York: privately printed, 1931), opposite p. 18.
3. Nathaniel Mason Pawlett, *Historic Roads of Virginia: Albemarle County Roads, 1725–1816* (Charlottesville: Virginia Highway and Transportation and Research Council, 1981), p. 75.
4. Copy of St. Anne's Parish Vestry Book, 1771–84 (Mss1B3445eFA2), Virginia Historical Society, Richmond; quoted by permission of St. Anne's Parish.
5. John Coles Account Book, 1775–76, p. 81 (acc. no. 3345), Manuscripts Department, University of Virginia Library.
6. Albemarle County Land Tax Books, 1782–98, microfilm reels 6 and 7, County Clerk's Office, Charlottesville, Va.
7. Thomas Jefferson had been influential in having this law repealed in the Virginia House of Delegates.
8. Records of building (Woodville) from John Coles Account Book, 1794–96, p. 194, University of Virginia Library.
9. Mutual Assurance Society Records, no. 351, vol. 13 (1799), Virginia Historic Landmarks Commission, Richmond. See also no. 691, vol. 15, reel 2 (1802), and no. 2274, vol. 45, reel 5 (1810).
10. John Coles Account Book, 1784–86, pp. 119, 122, 123, 124, University of Virginia Library.

11. Sarah Coles to Polly Coles, May 11, 1796, Smith-Carter Papers (acc. no. 1729), Manuscripts Department, University of Virginia Library.
12. John Coles Account Book, 1798, p. 158, University of Virginia Library.
13. Drucilla G. Haley, "Redlands: The Documentation of a Carter Plantation," masters thesis, University of Virginia, 1977, p. 10. The name West Oak was contributed by Mr. Robert Carter.
14. John Coles Account Book, 1798, p. 228, University of Virginia Library.
15. Haley, "Redlands," p. 9.

V

1. Isaac Coles to Joseph C. Cabell, Washington, Mar. 1807, private collection.
2. Rebecca Coles quoted in Elizabeth Langhorne, *Prestwould* (Clarksville, Va., 1982), a chap book of the Prestwould Foundation, p. 20.
3. Helen Coles to her sister Selina Skipwith, Enniscorthy, June 15, 1810, private collection.
4. Copy of will of Lady Skipwith in a letter from C. Johnson, attorney, to Col. John Coles, Aug. 28, 1826, private collection.
5. Luther Porter Jackson, *Free Negro Labor and Property Holding in Virginia, 1830–1860* (New York: D. Appleton Century, 1942), pp. 36, 37.
6. Elizabeth Coles, Diary, 1829 (Mss5:1C6795:1), Virginia Historical Society, Richmond.
7. Helen Coles to Lelia (Mrs. Humberston) Skipwith, Feb. 21, 1834, private collection.
8. Helen Coles to Selina Coles, June 13, 1835, private collection.
9. In a letter of recommendation obtained by Phillips in April of 1830, the writer, John Kelly, refers to Col. John Coles, "who has put up a splendid building just now completed, the brick work was done by Mr. Phillips" (Papers of Bishop John Early, Randolph Macon College, Ashland, Va.).
10. Calder Loth, report nominating Estouteville for the National Register of Historic Places, 1977, Historic Landmarks Commission, Richmond.
11. Isaac Coles to Gen. John Hartwell Cocke, Feb. 23, 1816, quoted in Peter Hodson, "The Design and Building of Bremo," master's thesis, University of Virginia, 1967.
12. William B. O'Neal, "The Workmen at the University of Virginia," *Magazine of Albemarle County History* 17 (1958–59): 11.
13. Helen Coles to Selina Coles, May 1828, private collection.
14. Helen to Selina, Baltimore, Monday, "May" 18, 1835, private collection.
15. Langhorne, *Prestwould*, p. 19. See also Catherine Lynn, *Wallpaper in America* (New York: W. W. Norton, 1980).
16. Report of plaster and paint analysis by Professor Laurence A. Pace, Virginia Commonwealth University, Richmond, Virginia, 1983.
17. Mark Girouard, *Life in the English Country House* (New York: Penguin Books, 1980), p. 164.
18. Helen to Selina, June 13, 1835, private collection. (Extracts are on file at the Maryland Historical Society.)
19. Helen to Selina, June 20 and July 2, 1835, private collection.
20. Helen to Selina, June 20, 1835, private collection.
21. Helen Coles quoted by the Rev. Roberts Coles in "The Coles Homes on the Green Mountain," unpublished typescript (ca. 1900), private collection, pp. 5, 6.
22. *Thomas Jefferson's Garden Book*, ed. Edwin Morris Betts (Philadelphia: American Philosophical Society, 1944), pl. 29.
23. Robert Beverly, *The History and Present State of Virginia* (London, 1705; reprint ed., Chapel Hill: University of North Carolina Press, 1947), p. 292.
24. Ellen Wayles Randolph to Martha Jefferson Randolph, Aug. 24, 1819, Coolidge-Jefferson Family Correspondence (acc. no. 9090), Manuscripts Department, University of Virginia Library.
25. Coles, "The Coles Homes," pp. 15, 16.
26. John Hartwell Cocke to Joseph C. Cabell, Bremo, Mar. 11, 1822, Cabell Papers (acc. no. 38–111), Manuscripts Department, University of Virginia Library.
27. Helen Coles quoted in Coles, "The Coles Homes."
28. Heather A. Clemenson, *English Country Houses and Landed Estates* (New York: St. Martin's Press, 1982).
29. Joseph C. Cabell to John Hartwell Cocke, Oct. 17, 1833, Cabell Papers (acc. no. 38–111), Manuscript Department, University of Virginia Library.
30. Will of Tucker Coles, 1861, Albermarle County Will Book 26, pp. 225–29, County Clerk's Office, Charlottesville, Va.

VI

1. Information from Mrs. Barbara Cabell Willcox, 1984.
2. Isaac Coles to Joseph C. Cabell, Jan. 23, 1802 (The first in a series of Coles-Cabell letters), private collection.
3. Coles to Cabell, July 15, 1804, private collection.

4. Coles to Cabell, Apr. 5, 1808, private collection.
5. Silvio A. Bedini, *Thomas Jefferson and His Copying Machines*, (Charlottesville: University Press of Virginia, 1984), p. 4.
6. Coles to Cabell, Apr. 5, 1808, private collection.
7. Coles to Cabell, Dec. 9, 1809, private collection.
8. Coles to Cabell, Jan. 29, 1811, private collection.
9. *Thomas Jefferson's Garden Book*, ed. Edwin Morris Betts (Philadelphia: American Philosophical Society, 1944), p. 525.
10. Coles to Cabell, Jan. 27, 1812, and Nov. 21, 1815, private collection.
11. Coles to Cabell, Nov. 5, 1916, private collection; Thomas Jefferson Memorandum Book, courtesy Ms. Lucia Stanton, Monticello, Charlottesville; Coles to Cabell, Aug. 1, 1819, private collection.
12. Martha Jefferson Randolph to Nicholas P. Trist, June 25, 1823, Nicholas P. Trist Papers, no. 2104, Southern Historical Collection, University of North Carolina, Chapel Hill.
13. Coles to Cabell, Aug. 29, 1831, private collection.
14. *The Writings of Thomas Jefferson*, Paul Leicester Ford, ed., 10:392–96. (New York: G. P. Putnam's Sons, 1905).
15. Edmund Bacon to Thomas Jefferson, Jan. 27, 1809, microfilm, reel 12, Coolidge Collection, Massachusetts Historical Society, Boston.
16. Coles to Cabell, July 25, 1832, private collection.
17. Coles to Cabell, Aug. 11, 1832, private collection.
18. Coles to Cabell, Feb. 25, 1810, private collection.
19. Ibid.

VII

1. Samuel Dyer to Tucker Coles, May 14, 1830, Smith-Carter Papers (acc. no. 1729), Manuscripts Department, University of Virginia Library.
2. Quoted from John S. Wyper, Jr., and Russell C. Scott, "Christ Church, Glendower, 1832," Studies in Vernacular Architecture, 1973, under the supervision of K. Edward Lay, typescript, Fiske Kimball Fine Arts Library, University of Virginia, unpaged addendum.
3. Ibid.
4. Jennie Thornley Grayson, "Old Christ Church, Charlottesville, Va., 1826–1895," *Papers of the Albemarle County Historical Society* 8 (1947–48): 33.
5. Bishop William Meade, *Old Churches, Ministers, and Families of Virginia* vol. 2 (Philadelphia: J. B. Lippincott & Co., 1900), p. 51, quoted in William Bedford Coles, *The Coles Family of Virginia* (New York: privately printed, 1931), p. 881.

VIII

1. Will of Rebecca Elizabeth Tucker Coles, Oct. 16, 1825, in Albemarle County Will Book 8, p. 242, County Clerk's Office, Charlottesville, Va. Proved July 3, 1826.
2. Elizabeth (Miss Betsy) Coles to John Coles III, The Hills, Feb. 14, 1827, private collection.
3. Edward Boykin, *Victoria, Albert, and Mrs. Stevenson* (New York: Rinehart and Co., 1957), p. 250.
4. "Rock Castle," *Bulletin of the Goochland County Historical Society* 1, no. 2 (Autumn 1969): 12, 13.
5. Correspondence with Henry Taylor of Taylor and Parrish, General Contractors, Richmond, Va. Mr. Taylor's firm moved Old Rock Castle in 1935 and executed measured drawings at that time. (See fig. 68b, c.)

IX

1. Will of Elizabeth Coles, 1865, Albemarle County Will Book 27, County Clerk's Office, Charlottesville, Va.
2. Helen Coles to Selina Coles, Philadelphia, May 13, 1828, private collection.
3. Edward Coles to unidentified correspondent, Apr. 1844, Edward Coles Papers, Historical Society of Pennsylvania, Philadelphia, p. A4.
4. Amherst County Deed Book E, p. 605, Virginia State Library, Richmond.
5. Edward Coles to unidentified correspondent, Apr. 1844, Edward Coles Papers, Historical Society of Pennsylvania, Philadelphia, p. A7.
6. Edward Coles to John Coles, Washington, May 6, 1812, Historical Society of Pennsylvania, Philadelphia.
7. Edward Coles to John Coles, Brownsville, Pa., Apr. 11, 1819, Smith-Carter Papers (acc. no. 1729), Manuscripts Department, University of Virginia Library.
8. Edward Coles to unidentified correspondent, Apr. 1844, Edward Coles Papers, Historical Society of Pennsylvania, Philadelphia, p. A27.
9. Ibid., p. A30.
10. Edward Coles to James Madison, 1819, James Madison Papers (acc. no. 2988), Manuscripts Department, University of Virginia Library.
11. Edward Coles Account Books, quoted in notes by Donald Fremont Lewis, furnished by Roger D. Bridges, Illinois State Historical Library, Springfield.
12. Edward Coles, "Sketch Describing the Emancipation of the Slaves of Edward Coles" (n.d.), Edward Coles Papers, Historical Society of Pennsylvania, Philadelphia, p. B10.

13. Deed registered July 4, 1819, in the Office of the Recorder, Madison County, Ill., quoted in notes by Donald Fremont Lewis, furnished by Roger D. Bridges, Illinois State Historical Library, Springfield.
14. Robert "Preacher" Crawford to Edward Coles, Oct. 23, 1846, quoted in notes by Donald Fremont Lewis, furnished by Roger D. Bridges, Illinois State Historical Library, Springfield.
15. Roberts Coles to friend, Camp Defiance, Oct. 13, 1861 (Mss1R933763), Virginia Historical Society, Richmond.
16. Roberts Coles to Jenny Cary Fairfax, Feb. 7, 1862 (Mss2C6799a1), Virginia Historical Society, Richmond.
17. Edward Coles to Col. John Rutherfoord, Oct. 1861, box 2, folder 23, Edward Coles Papers, Princeton University Library. Published with permission of Princeton University Library.

X

1. William Bedford Coles, *The Coles Family of Virginia* (New York: privately printed, 1931), p. 99.
2. James Madison to Edward Coles, Oct. 3, 1834, James Madison Papers (acc. no. 2988), Manuscripts Department, University of Virginia Library.
3. Deed Book 39, p. 372, Albemarle County Clerks Office, Charlottesville, Va.
4. Miss Betsy Coles to Mrs. Sally Carter Randolph (Mrs. Benjamin Franklin), Richmond, Mar. 29, 1836, Smith-Carter Papers (acc. no. 1729), Manuscripts Department, University of Virginia Library.
5. Miss Betsy to John Coles III, Georgetown, July 17, 1824, private collection.
6. James Alexander, *Early Charlottesville*, ed. Mary Rawlings (Charlottesville, Va.: Peoples Bank, 1942), p. 28.
7. Coles, *The Coles Family*, pp. 694, 695, 753–55.

Index

(C) 1808: c. 7,000 contiguous acres in Albemarle at the time of John II's death. Total acreage acquired by John III, 14,475½ acres, including some 7,475 acres outside the home tracts.

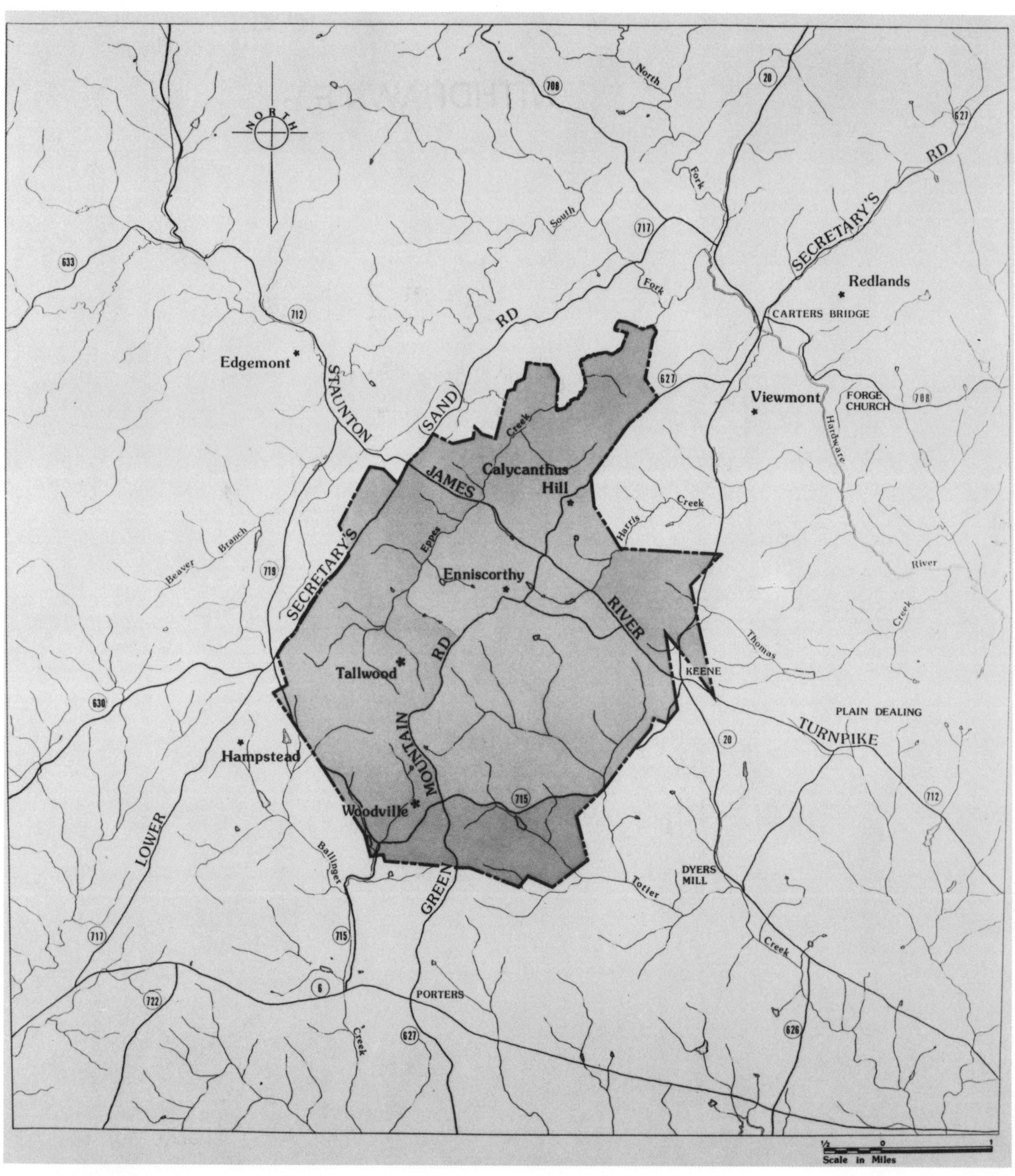